The greatest mystery of the universe is the secret of our souls. Edgar Cayce delved deeply into questions of where we come from, how our decisions, our work, relationships, and futures are shaped by forces we cannot always perceive. In this extraordinary work, Lin Cochran examines Cayce's teachings and shows how you can learn to:

- Understand—and accept—the teachings of your own higher intelligence.
- Follow twelve principles for revealing the truth of your secret self.
- Find new meaning for your life in Edgar Cayce's revolutionary interpretations of the Bible.
- Uncover the secret laws that govern your relationships with family, lovers, and friends.
- Follow the path of prosperity by giving to—and accepting from—others.

In an age of change, stress, and instant communication, this work reveals the channels between your consciousness and the laws of the universe you are a part of—and the way to a more peaceful, fulfilling future.

EDGAR CAYCE
ON SECRETS OF THE UNIVERSE AND HOW TO USE THEM IN YOUR LIFE

Books in The Edgar Cayce Series

EDGAR CAYCE

ON SECRETS OF THE UNIVERSE AND HOW TO USE THEM IN YOUR LIFE

BY LIN COCHRAN
UNDER THE EDITORSHIP OF
CHARLES THOMAS CAYCE

WARNER BOOKS

A Warner Communications Company

WARNER BOOKS EDITION

Copyright © 1989 by the Association for Research and
Enlightenment, Inc.
All rights reserved.

Cover design by Karen Katz

Warner Books, Inc.
666 Fifth Avenue
New York, N.Y. 10103

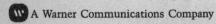 A Warner Communications Company

Printed in the United States of America

First Printing: April, 1989

10 9 8 7 6 5 4 3 2 1

Dedicated with thanks to

My beloved Thomas
who is overcoming his doubts

to A. Robert Smith
who is overcoming mine

to Everett Irion
who never had any doubts that I know of

and

to Dorothy FitzGerald
who listens to all of it

Contents

Who Was Edgar Cayce?

Of all the psychics known in modern times, Edgar Cayce is perhaps the most carefully documented, believable, and remarkable. Widely known today through the dozens of books published about his work, Edgar Cayce was born in Kentucky in 1877 and died in Virginia in 1945. Throughout his life he was guided by a desire to use his unusual abilities for the benefit of others.

While he was a young man, Cayce found his career as a salesman nearly ruined by a seemingly incurable loss of voice. But curious abilities came to his aid. While under hypnosis, he spoke normally, diagnosing his ailment and prescribing a simple treatment that was effective. He later discovered that he was able to enter a deep trance state and from this state give discourses on virtually any question or topic. The transcripts of his discourses are called "readings."

Twice a day for more than forty years, Cayce would lie down, enter this self-induced hypnotic state and, given only the name and location of his subject, describe in detail the functionings and malfunctionings of his or her body, no matter where in the world the person was at the time. Following his diagnosis came a prescription for treatment of the condition. Then came a period of questions and answers which supplied other needed information.

The terminology Cayce used in his diagnoses was so advanced it often sent doctors to their medical dictionaries. His therapies included an impressive array of treatments including osteopathy, chiropractic, hydrotherapy, chemotherapy, massage and diet. His answers and advice always stressed the necessity of a balanced, well-rounded life in which body, mind and spirit functioned as a coordinated unit. They were especially remarkable in light of the fact that Cayce had only a grade school education, knew nothing about medicine, and neither heard nor remembered anything he said while asleep.

Even more astounding was the sleeping Cayce's accuracy:

of those cases verified by patients' reports, at least 85% of the diagnoses were found to be completely accurate; and those patients who followed the prescribed treatments got the results predicted in the reading. Some truly remarkable cures came about as a result of Cayce's advice. In one instance, he gave a reading for a man who had lost his family and job and been confined to an insane asylum for three years following a nervous breakdown. The reading explained that "through pressure upon the lumbar axis, there has been a deflection of coordination between the sympathetic and the cerebrospinal nervous system." Rather than nervous tension, the breakdown was attributed to a spinal injury caused by a fall years earlier. What was required was not psychotherapy but osteopathic adjustment and a mild, specially outlined electrotherapy to normalize the disrupted nerve forces. Cayce's suggested treatment was followed and the results were dramatic. Within six months the man had fully recovered, was reunited with his family, and reinstated in his job.

For many years the information requested of Edgar Cayce was related mainly to physical ills. The repeated accuracy of his diagnoses and the effectiveness of the sometimes unorthodox treatments he prescribed made him a medical phenomenon. The fact that he needed only the name and current location of an individual anywhere in the world to give a searching diagnosis of his or her physical condition compounded the mystery.

But the information that came through Cayce was not limited to physical subjects. It was discovered that Cayce's source of information was virtually unlimited. Given the proper suggestion, he could and did speak with authority on a vast range of subjects. The only apparent limitation of this source of information was that it provided only that information which was in the best interests of those concerned. For example, in attempting to locate a missing person, it became apparent that the missing man didn't want to be located. Cayce indicated that the man was alive and briefly sketched his activities, assuring his family that they could be reunited but he insisted that the decision to return must be made by the missing man, who had run away to escape family problems. Those problems, Cayce said, must be solved by those concerned—and simply locating the missing man would aggravate the situation, not help it. Eventually, the scope of his work expanded to include information and advice on thousands of subjects.

Edgar Cayce on Secrets of the Universe and How to Use Them in Your Life provides new insights into this aspect of the Edgar Cayce readings.

—Charles Thomas Cayce, Ph.D.

1

Stalking the Secrets

The secrets of the universe elude us. But we are gaining on them.

From the moment of creation until a moment ago, as we count time, much of our universe has remained hidden to our physical, naked eyes. Unaided by technology, human vision is limited when measured against what is really there before us. But thanks to computers that make it possible for scientists to see our world in a new way, and to television that makes it possible for us to see what the scientists see, we are becoming quite nonchalant about looking at images undreamed of even fifty years ago. We treat viewing the inside of a five-thousand-year-old mummy's brain cell, magnified twenty-five thousand times, as though it were an everyday occurrence.

We are becoming a nation of educational-television junkies, glued to our sets, fascinated by the world inside us and around us, so recently visible for the first time. We are easily mesmerized by us. Nothing is more interesting than we are—our bodies, our planet, our galaxy. We crave to know how it all works. Television is beginning to show us how much we know and how much we don't know.

One recent fifty-minute segment shown on public television, titled *The Infinite Voyage*,[1] presented artists and scientists coming together to create pictures of the world never before seen. We were shown how an artist, by assigning different colors to the elements of atoms, modeling their location and exposing them to computer-generated sunlight, makes it possible for a scientist to measure subtle shifts and changes in molecules unseen before. The narrator said the molecular engine that converts sunlight into energy, the process of photosynthesis, has become visible. Scientists can actually see the workings of the chemical factory that supports life on earth. And so can we.

We were told that artists and scientists are now looking at the two sides of the coin as if they were the same. And to prove the point we were shown a computer so powerful it can read the entire Manhattan phone book in a fraction of a second, but that is useless until an artist, using the data, images mysterious objects in space. It takes art and science both to show television images of regions far beyond our solar system, where astronomers have captured a faint picture of two great oceans of superheated gas. The narrator said that until now, little detail of this cosmic blowtorch could be seen. But there in our living rooms, the dynamics of the powerful jet emerged, driven by the physical laws that govern this universe.

Computer modeling allows scientists to share information

[1]*The Infinite Voyage, Unseen Worlds,* narrated by Richard Kiley. A production of WQED, Pittsburgh, in association with the National Academy of Sciences.

with each other. And television allows them to share their discoveries with us. And together, we marvel at the complex processes that shape our planet.

Of considerable interest are radio-wave pictures of stars being born, much in the same way our own sun was created some 4½ billion years ago. But one of the most impressive and rarest sights to be seen in our galaxy—which, we were told, has been seen only five times in the past 900 years— is the death of a star called the supernova. Yet there it was, depicted in living color.

The wonder seems to be that radio waves were discovered at all in this universe filled with violence, pulsars whirling around, and natural disasters, as the total energy of all radio waves ever recorded barely equals the force of a single snowflake. Still, thanks to radio waves, a cosmic hurricane has been located in the center of our own galaxy, the Milky Way. And our sight has been extended into galaxies that lie far beyond our own by the ingenious array of dishes that turn sound into pictures. Who does not agree with, "How we see our universe will never be the same"?

Astronomers track and plot a thousand far-flung galaxies a million times dimmer than the stars we see at night for the first three-dimensional map of the universe. They pose questions about the newly discovered architecture of the planets and stars that make up our solar system; and we get to play "what if?" alongside some of the top minds in the country. It satisfies a childlike curiosity in us.

In further childlike amazement we can only wonder about the newest toy of the micro world—a scanning, tunneling microscope that holds a needle 10 million times smaller than a human hair. Just how small is that, anyway?

And yet we learn the irony that scientists must use a four-story-high microscope to find the smallest things there are: how can a piece of silicon be a million times smaller than the head of a pin? Is that smaller than the electron shells of individual atoms? How about the bonds that hold the atoms together? There on the TV screen are all of these dramatic images.

Then, like little kids enraptured by *Sesame Street*, we stare at radio signals from human space, created by magnetic resonance imaging, which is said to realign the atoms within the human body, while a surgeon plots his strategy for repairing the damaged brain before him.

Medical pioneers, we are told and shown, have made it possible to use three-dimensional x-rays to peer inside the spinal column. Shoulder joints can be separated through imagery and inspected for hidden fractures, all without invading the body of the patient. Doctors can now see the inside of the heart without injecting dye into it through a needle. Electronic diagnosis through the use of three-dimensional motion pictures will make the old poke-and-wait method obsolete.

Suddenly everything seems obsolete, as if all that *was* is gone, and what *is* awaits fresh, willing-to-learn eyes.

Leon Lederman, head of Illinois's Fermi Particle Accelerator Laboratory, explains that we all start out curious: "Little kids, as soon as they learn to talk, they're all scientists. They ask exactly the right questions. They say, 'Why is the sky blue?' Or they say, 'What keeps a bird up in the air?' They keep asking questions. Parents shouldn't get upset because they send them to school, and pretty soon the teachers in the school will beat all the stuff out of them, and they'll all cue to a more sensible line, and they'll stop asking questions, and they'll grow up to be good, useful citizens—lawyers and postmen and so on. But a few of them will be ornery. They'll refuse to grow up, and they'll be physicists, or maybe even poets."

In Illinois, Lederman's team of scientists crashes protons, then studies the resulting quarks, the smallest particles known, in hopes of finding even smaller particles.

Any curious kid who looks up the word "quark" in a dictionary that's more than a few years old will learn that a quark was recently considered to be hypothetical. Meanwhile, with every question that is answered, a new one appears, another detail to be explored in the search for how it all works.

But if the secrets of the outer world elude us, what of those of the inner world? If we had an eight-story-high microscope, could we see the soul? With a larger array of telescopic dishes, would the radio waves show us the face of God? Will we ever be able to see not brain but mind?

Edgar Cayce said everything without is within; everything that resides in the heavens resides in the earth; that the planets and stars, as well as our bodies, are corpuscles in the body of God; that it is all one.

If scientists are not finished asking questions of the universe without, how do we hope to fathom the secrets of the universe within? Cayce said we live our way into the understanding of it, line by line, precept upon precept; and that knowledge is irrelevant, even destructive, if we don't act on what we already know.

During the first half of the century scientists sought the secrets to outer space flight. The last half of the century is being spent applying previous lessons learned, and learning new ones. The search for the secrets of inner space is equally real. Inner-journey voyagers are a network of soul scientists, sharing the discovery of laws and principles which govern a vista of unknowns. The puzzle is beginning to reveal a picture which we are realizing will never be complete until each one adds his piece. The purpose of this effort is to shine a light on the puzzle, better to see how each piece fits.

The principles aren't particularly complicated. In fact, it's their confounded simplicity that makes them difficult. We know more about how spiritual principles work than why they work. Violate one too often and we never get off the launching pad.

Almost everybody agrees the world feels like it's in a countdown to blast off. Anticipation of something wonderful is palpable. But it's the inner world that's trembling. There's a quiet exuberance vibrating across the land. Many feel like children, knowing in their hearts there really is a Santa Claus. Others are afraid to believe but desperately want to.

All of us are in search of our own secrets. Here is my hope for you finding yours:

> May the Father speak,
> Spirit move,
> and Light come into your world.

Live innocently. God is here.
—Carl von Linné[1]

2

Secrets of Soul Guidance

Your soul is your secret, psychic self. In fact, *psychic* means "of the soul." It represents the part of you that existed in God's mind before the world was. And it has a job to do. It is trying to get home. But first, you discover why it came here. When you allow your soul to guide you, your secret self, then, has its life. Your secret self is the real, unselfish you. Selfishness blocks the gift of guidance your soul wants to give you. But that can be changed.

The person you are today did not drop full-blown out of a tree this morning. You worked faithfully and diligently to

[1] 1707–1778, *Linnaeus*, Ib. 15, inscribed over the door of Linnaeus's bedchamber.

7

bring about the circumstances, situations, and persons in your life. You built your existence out of the stuff life is made of: your ideals, attitudes, and emotions toward people, places, things, and events, and your concept of God. And spirit gives your existence life.

You have form. You exist in space. You experience time. You live in relation to something and someone. You are individual. You agree with some things, disagree with others. You feel complete or incomplete, joined or separated. You live in some degree of order or disorder, harmony or disharmony. You had a beginning, you are living in the middle, and you as you know yourself will have an end. Then the real you will continue or discontinue. You know unity and duality, limits and limitlessness. You experience seasons, change, permanence. You are powerful and impotent, productive and unproductive. You are skin and bone and blood and mind and spirit. You have a front, a back, a right, a left, an up, a down, and a sideways. You are sharp and blunt, smooth and rough, open and closed. You are physics, heat, light, electricity, mechanics, color, sound, and music. And you matter.

What you *do* matters.

Your intellectual faculties, intelligence, comprehension, reasoning processes, considerations, assessments, conclusions, theories, beliefs, and grounds for those beliefs do *not* matter *unless* your life works.

A life that works means your relationships with yourself and others work. It means you love yourself and someone else. And at least one living person—age and sex irrelevant— loves you back. It means you are not trapped in self-defeating patterns and reactions to the past. It means every or almost every day is met with joy in the work to be done. It means regular, fresh intake of information to help you in that work, friends with whom to interact, feedback, and shared victories and defeats. It's a higher source than yourself to communicate with daily, balanced health maintenance, and playtime.

If your life works it is because of your secret self's ideal.

If your life doesn't work it is because of your known self's ideal.

The ideal is what has been motivating you. If it isn't working for you, change it.

But it must be said right here that changing how you feel or think will not change your life. Changing what you *do* will change your life, as well as how you feel and think.

A way to change what you do is to discover the secret self's ideal.

Here is the collective ideal for all the secret selves:

That each one of us fulfills the purpose for which we were born.

What does that mean?

That we each have a job to do and a mutual reason for doing it.

It isn't really complicated. That's what makes it so difficult.

It may be as simple as getting acquainted with the real you and discovering the desires of your true nature. Your desires—which govern absolutely—are either selfish or unselfish. We are all either secret-self centered or known-self centered. It is vital to discover where we are with selfishness and unselfishness because some degree of those two is all there is. Selfishness and unselfishness make up the warp and woof of our individuality. Everyone is becoming one or the other. Which are you gradually becoming?

Selfishness concerns itself with one's own welfare regardless of others, gives less than the best to others, and may take the form of self-aggrandizement, self-glory, self-centeredness, self-abasement, self-doubt, and many other "self" words, including self-control. Selfishness encompasses smugness, complacency, egotism, narcissism, conceit, perfectionism, arrogance, manipulation, denial, avoidance, fears, false pride, pretension, hypocrisy, pomposity, mistrust, condescension, indifference, presumptuousness, expectations, martyrdom, addictions, ambition, possessiveness, weakness, greed, and control of others.

Unselfishness, besides being the opposite of the above, is

giving generously to one's self *as well as* others *for all the right reasons*. It is being good when no one's watching, caring longer than anybody, loving anyway. Unselfishness is doing what you know to do even when you don't feel like it. It's not giving in to the impulse of the moment. It's not making excuses for your own or anybody else's failure. It's taking responsibility for what you are responsible for—and absolutely nothing else. It's letting everybody do their own growing in spite of caring that they hurt. It's not letting them hurt alone. It's intimate honesty and honestly intimate. It's letting others know what you want from them. It's lovingly letting go if they can't give it.

Consider this: You are sick and need a ride to the doctor. I give it to you. Am I selfish or unselfish? The answer depends on why I gave it to you.

A network of selfish motives could make me say yes, starting with the fear of saying no to you because you won't like me if I do. Too, I could be looking for self-glory. If it makes me feel good to aid sick little you, that's selfishness. If I drive you because then I can expect you to drive me when I'm sick, that's self. If I use the opportunity to belittle your unhealthy life style as why you are sick, that's self. If driving you is an excuse to get out of doing something else, that's self. In fact, about the only way I can drive you to the doctor at all without some element of self getting into the act is to call you a taxi. But I did drive you, and I used it as an opportunity to observe where, in being a samaritan, I am behaving selfishly or unselfishly. By helping you I knew myself better. I came a bit closer to fulfilling the purpose for which I was born: to allow the secret self to have its life, to grow toward being unselfish, to live out its ideal.

We don't wake up one morning suddenly unselfish. We grow or climb up. As Cayce so aptly put it, "You don't hop off a ladder up on the upper boughs! You grow, you climb up."

Watch a vine. Delicate tendrils reach and stretch, often flailing the air for something on which to catch hold. Without an ideal, we are like a vine without a trellis. Watch a child climb a tree, looking up, reaching upward for the next limb. That's us living the secret self's ideal.

But to suggest that we are ever *without* an ideal is erroneous. We may have no idea what it is, and when we find it we may call it something else, but we can't get into earth without one. The ideal is the two-way ticket that gets us a seat on the soul train headed this way. Purpose is the *what* we have to do; the ideal is the *why.*

Cayce said we aren't allowed into earth without an ideal. Your soul knows what it is, and will guide you into the purpose for which you were born.

Fulfilling the purpose for which you were born has to do somehow with your relationship *with* and your concept *of* God.

Great worldly achievements don't count for much in the real world, the *inner* world. Love is in the little things. The Bible asks what have we gained if we gain the whole world and lose our souls? Our souls are infinitely more interested in how we spend our money than how much of it sits in the bank. In our Father's house are many mansions, and you and I are two of them.

If your purpose is mired in speculation and doubt, and you don't know why you are here, you cheat yourself out of the guidance your soul wants to give you, and you cheat your soul out of its chance to get home, as well as its relationship with the Creator.

Your purpose is related somehow to your attitudes and emotions about people, places, things, and events. We are each here to start something, finish something, clean up, eliminate, correlate, or incorporate *something* related to people, places, or things, and events of the past, the future, or this very moment. And it all somehow relates to your understanding of your God. Here's how to find out how it relates.

Guidance Through Discovery of the Secret Self

Get a pencil and paper. Ask three questions:

> What did I come here to do?
> Why do I need to do that?
> How do I go about doing it?

Begin where you are. You can't get someplace else unless you begin here. Write the question, "What did I come here to do?" Take a deep breath, and from the space between breathing in and breathing out, begin to write. Don't censor, judge, or evaluate. Just write.

Feeling resistance to writing? That's your subconscious feeling threatened. If you give in, it will keep you in its grip. A peculiar thing about the subconscious mind is that it seems to be rendered inoperative from the space between breathing in and breathing out. It feels as though you've drawn a curtain that covers it and at the same time reveals the soul mind.

Your answer may take the form of forty pages of unleashed passion, or it may consist of three words, such as "To know me." In that case, the question, then, is *Who is the "me"?* So pose that question and answer it, again, from the space between breathing in and breathing out. In fact, all self-knowledge writing should be carried out from this space, simply because it's the most effective. You can trust information from this space to be relevant. If you allow the subconscious and conscious minds to get into the act, you'll wear out your hand and wind up with little more than excuses and rationalizations why you *aren't* living your purpose and getting guidance from your soul.

After getting the answer to the first question, ask: "Why do I need to do that?" Breathe deeply and let flow the first thing that comes to mind. Don't be concerned with how the words read. Let your soul find its own voice. Don't try to manipulate the words to fit someone else's norm. Trying to fit someone else's norm is probably part of your problem, so let that one go.

Then ask, "How do I go about doing it?"

Again, breathe deeply and—without qualifying—write the answer. If your life isn't working, it may come in the form of "Read that book over there on the shelf." However, if your life is working, you may get something like, "Just keep on keeping on. You're headed in the right direction."

Mostly our lives work in some areas but not in others. So you may want to apply the questions to specific areas most unsatisfying. It's perfectly okay to start in one particular area, rather than generalize about your whole life. After all, the purpose here is guidance where you need it most through discovery of the secret self.

Keep your questions positive, such as, "Why am I in this relationship?" or "Why am I in this job?" Don't ask, "Why doesn't anything ever work out the way I want it to?" Your subconscious will—I guarantee—bash you to smithereens. Or, worse still, the subconscious will hand you answers such as, "It's all so-and-so's fault. If it weren't for him or her . . ."

If self-knowledge writing is carried out in the right way, your soul will speak to you of its need to have its life. Your soul is waiting its turn to guide you.

The point is, however, to *do* whatever the answer says because it's works, not words, that get the job done. Following soul guidance results in having more inner guidance, more communication from your soul. Step by step, the path you must take stretches before you. It may lead you into small-group work, various therapies and recovery programs, church, prayer, meditation, volunteer work, and on and on, bringing to you the right people, places, things, and events that will lead you into living your purpose. When you're living your purpose, you're living your ideal. It's easier to live the *what* if you know the *why*.

The secret self's ideal is not a list of shoulds and oughts. It's your motivator. No one can tell you what that is. Some have found that establishing a theme for life leads to clearer focus on the secret self's ideal.

Certain words and phrases help define the theme. This theme, this unifying or dominant idea, can help you live the ideal, and it's never too late to start. No matter what your heredity and environment have been, you can begin where you are to let it work for you instead of against you.

One way to look at themes, and keep them sorted from ideals and purposes, is to see themes as "I am..." statements. The theme for your life does not necessarily concern your occupation, though it may. Probably, the theme can be stated abstractly. If, for example, you choose as a theme, *I am an enhancer of beauty,* your occupation might be book-keeper, but your hobby gardening. Certainly a person who chooses a career of, say, hairstyling, who thinks of herself or himself as an enhancer of beauty, would be living a type of joyous oneness daily. If you're retired, or otherwise unemployed, the theme can follow your interests, and could be expressed simply as *I am helpful.* But "I am" statements don't specify what, why, and how to do.

Stay with the hairstylist for a moment and see the whole picture:

The theme: I am an enhancer of beauty.

The purpose (the what): My purpose for being born is to help others express their own individual beauty.

The secret self's ideal (the why): Creative service.

With the ideal of creative service, the *how* would natural-ly extend to other areas of life, not limit itself just to the job. Creative service is a form of unselfishness. A person living creative service as an ideal looks for ways to serve creatively. This person would not only drive you to the doctor, but would deliberately lay aside her own cares and think of ways to make you laugh during the trip. She would value greatly those few hours spent with you and would be grateful you asked for her help.

Your soul wants to guide you away from selfishness. The secret self's ideal always involves some type of unselfish service to others. We all can think of people who never seem to give a thought to spiritual development, but who are the most loving servants on earth. The blessed ones happily live outer-directed lives of service, totally unaware of a spiritual ideal. Maybe they know a secret the rest of us don't know. But we can learn.

Even when we are almost totally inner focused, such as when we are overcoming addictions, cleaning up our own act is an act of service to others. Seeing ourselves as others see us, then making corrections, is a service. When I make myself better—for whatever reason—you benefit, and vice versa. It's virtually impossible to help yourself without helping someone else. When I recognize my purpose for being here, I help you to see yours. Whether I use words such as "unselfish creative service" or "to be more like Christ," *if* I'm living it, not just talking about it, you can see it. If I only talk about it, I sound like a child banging on a garbage can with a hammer. I have to be it. If you can see it in someone else, that means you have it in yourself, for we are nothing if not mirrors of the secret self for one another.

You can also see it if I'm selfish. Again, I am mirroring you. Maybe my actions serve as a bad example. Don't hate me for showing you *you*. If you judge me, you judge yourself. If I threaten you, make you uncomfortable, shake your status quo, I'm probably unintentionally doing you a favor by giving you a chance to know yourself better.

When you begin to know your secret self's ideal, you can see the ideal your known self has been serving. If you can see it, you can change it.

If some area of your life isn't working, admit to yourself that the ideal you have been serving is some variation on the theme of selfishness.

All selfishness is a type of sin. All *evil* is a type of selfishness. All selfishness is sinful and evil. When the Bible talks about sin and evil, it's referring to selfishness. "For all have sinned and fallen short of the glory of God . . ." means all have been selfish at one time or another.

The secret self is the spiritual level of self. But there are two other levels: the physical and the mental. Ideals operate at all three levels. Ideals motivate. We serve the motivator. For instance, if money motivates, we serve the ideal of money. If power motivates, we serve the ideal of power. If success motivates, we serve the ideal of success. Now, money, power, and success are fine as results, but as motivators, they can be selfish. If your secret self desires money, power, and success so you can make the world a better place, then money, power, and success aren't your motivators. Service is. And only you know which is which.

Selfishness exacts a price physically, mentally, and spiritually. To illustrate:

Physically, serving the ideal of gluttony could be costing you your health as well as your happiness.

Mentally, serving the ideal of reason could be costing you peace of mind, for intellectualizing just won't account for much of what life is all about.

Spiritually, serving the ideal of man-made theology could be costing you soul development. Your soul could be sleeping through all those sermons.

Being unselfish helps on all three levels.

On the physical level, serving the ideal of well-being could restore or maintain health by making you diligently practice healthy habits.

On the mental level, serving the ideal of faith could clear up mental confusion about why the world seems so complex.

On the spiritual level, serving the ideal of courage could enable you to find a more personal relationship with your God.

So, by consciously replacing gluttony, reason, and man-made theology with well-being, faith, and courage, you do not stop eating, thinking, and attending church. Instead you eat, think, and attend services with a different purpose. You begin to view things from a new perspective, but the new perspective must be accompanied by different actions.

For instance, adopting a physical ideal of well-being means you stop giving in to self-indulgent impulses of the moment, and you start selecting better food. This requires time and effort. It means you spend time working out and sleeping. It means you allow yourself to play, to read, to listen to music, or whatever else contributes to your sense of well-being.

Adopting a mental ideal of faith means you give up worrying. You no longer spend time in fruitless conversational exchanges with fellow intellectuals in the pursuit of sanity. Instead, you identify one area of this complex world where you can do some good and volunteer to do it. You release emotional attachments to scholarship and begin to live your way into true understanding.

Adopting a spiritual ideal of courage means you dare to ask questions. It means you no longer accept what is told without researching it for yourself. You give to the quest time and energy because you dare risk learning.

These are examples of how actions affect thinking and feeling. Of course, a degree of thinking precedes any action, but it's a mistake to wait until you feel spiritually strong and courageous before asking questions. And it's silly to think any degree of well-being can be achieved while you are still practicing gluttony. Understanding follows *doing* rather than *intellectualizing*. You can't learn to play a piano by talking about it. And you can't receive soul guidance for selfish purposes. Trying to use soul power to harm another is to commit soul suicide.

Your soul will be tortured if you misuse its power. It will withdraw, maybe even banish itself. Your secret self longs to glorify its Creator. It cries when separated from the Father's love. It aches to return home. It knows the way home is to fulfill its mission. Don't deny your secret self its life.

Practicing the Principles of the Secret Self

Allowing the secret self to have its life is a process that requires new actions. New actions are generally accompanied by feeling a need for self-control. The Cayce readings suggest a better way: *Don't control. Patrol.*

Self-control implies a lot of breast-beating and condemnation for not having enough. On the other hand, *self-patrol* implies a constant evaluation of where we are in the process. You see, it's the process itself that will effect the changes. The principles of the process have been set into place and have been proven to work time and again. The principles work if we work the principles. Patrol is the principle of self-observation for the purpose of maintaining order and security. Order and security are found in the process.

Living the secret self's ideal can be summed up in five P's:

Practice
Principles
Process
Purpose
Patrol

You practice the principles, which lead you through the process, which deepens your understanding of your purpose. Then don't control. Patrol.

The better you get at practicing the principles daily, the better your life gets and the more the truth of the secret self is revealed.

What are the principles?

1. I alone am responsible for my reactions to people, places, things, events, situations, and circumstances.

2. I meet with my God in the temple of my body daily for communion, correction, and thanksgiving. I speak to God in prayer and listen to God in meditation. I open my heart and my hands to receive and send gifts of the Spirit. I read something daily to strengthen my faith.

3. I recognize every person I meet as an opportunity to serve God and to know myself better. Every person I meet is both student and teacher. I acknowledge their divinity as well as my own. The ground on which we both stand is holy.

4. Each day is set before me life and death, good and evil. In all things I choose life.

5. I love as I want to be loved, forgive as I want to be forgiven, give as I want to receive.

6. I obey universal laws as I understand them, in recognition that as I use what I have, more will be given.

7. I remain open to a deeper understanding of my purpose.

8. My words and actions agree with my purpose as I understand it.

9. I follow my soul guidance to individuals and to groups, acknowledging that God speaks to me through other people.

10. I claim my inheritance of will, faith, and freedom, and spend it on lights for the path of another, acknowledging bountiful abundance that multiplies in *all* matters.

11. I get out of my secret self's way and allow my soul to express what my mind has built in daily living and in dreams, which I record. I patrol myself but no one else, admit my errors to myself and others, and make corrections with God's help.

12. I surrender daily the victories and defeats of the past and future. I live in the reality of the moment.

Review the principles daily and evaluate by your own standards how you're doing. Living these principles is the process of living the secret self's ideal, by whichever words you choose to define it. By identifying and writing, in your own words, your secret self's ideal, you give your known self a link with the process. Your desire to *have* something or to *be* something is your motivator, your ideal.

You may write, "I will practice the principles because my secret self's ideal is *peace of mind*."

Tomorrow you may change it to, "I will practice the principles because my secret self's ideal is *to be a channel of God's love in the earth*."

Next week you may relate to another expression: "I will practice the principles because my secret self's ideal is *joy*."

Behind all these different expressions is some form of *unselfishness*. In reality the final, ultimate purpose each one of us is born for is to get beyond the personality—the known, outer *self*—all the way to the Christ. We gradually peel layers of selfishness to reveal and glorify the God within. But because we are all different, and our experiences of heredity, environment, mind, and spirit are uniquely our own, the method we choose to shed the outer layers, and the words we choose to express our secret self must be our own. But express it we must.

Where is the downside in all this? It's the will. Only by conscious willing and willingness are the inner secrets of the soul revealed.

Mark Thurston calls the secret self "the true identity, the individuality, the spiritual I." In *Paradox of Power* he writes, "The individuality... the spiritual 'I' which has continuity from lifetime to lifetime... is not yet perfected but it is capable of growth and development." (p. 176)

In this excellent book, the best of many available on ideals and purpose, Thurston breaks new ground in the area of the human will. He explains why—even though the principles are in place—staying in the process of allowing the secret self to have its life and living the ideal can be difficult.

"An ideal is a deeply felt motivator for living, not an intellectual abstraction that says 'ought' or 'should.' An ideal invites and holds attention because it evokes reinforcing feelings which make attention more likely to remain in place.

"However, as straightforward and simple as all of this may sound, most people have very little capacity to concentrate... because the will is asleep."

The will of the secret self begins to awaken through practicing the principles. The more the will awakens, the deeper the understanding of the process at work.

Meditation furthers awakening. If you are meditating, as many are, for relaxation, lowering blood pressure, and healing ulcers, why not awaken the secret self and transform your life while you're at it? (I'm not sure that learning to meditate won't transform your life even if you aren't trying. It could be that learning to relax is the transformer. I don't think the genie cares by what means it gets out of the bottle.)

Most doctors won't say in so many words "learn meditation, awaken your secret self, change your relationship with God, yourself, and others. Then your soul will begin to guide you and you'll feel better." You'd accuse him or her of preaching without a license. A doctor's responsibility is to relieve symptoms, not to alter theology. But something similar to modern medicine's "revolutionary techniques" of hypnosis and biofeedback, which, in actuality, are as old as mankind—and only recently have required machines—definitely plays a role in spiritual awakening.

The major difference between meditation for relaxation and meditating for spiritual awakening and soul guidance is purpose. Either way you probably receive a large dose of psychoneuroimmunology, the mind-body link to strengthening the immune system, which is intertwined with endocrinology and clinical nutrition, as well as relaxation techniques. Shifting the focus away from the known—the lower self and mere relaxation—to the unknown secret self and service to others, awakens the desire to be used for good.

When we begin to know in whom the secret self believes, doors open. We begin to recognize Spirit, but more so, know that we are recognized by Spirit as channels of joy, peace, and happiness. Spirit moves like a stream throughout our bodies. But a stream with no outlet becomes stagnant and impure. So to keep it flowing, give it out. When your soul begins to guide you, have faith in yourself as one of the beloved.

Be the light, and remember, doubt shuts it out. Doubt is a call to prayer. Pray, "Help thou my unbelief." (262-11)

When the soul is guiding, expect truth. Truth is like the ocean. Only the surface can be seen. Expect to be swept along by oceans of truth, in rushes, flats, and valleys, peaks, highs, and lows. At each moment, truth is experienced from our own perspective.

Expect love. Love is like a prayer: *Show me the best of myself and I will love you.* Be the answer to someone's prayer and yours will be answered.

Expect power. Power is like wind. A hurricane is but a gentle breeze gone mad. Be the eye in someone's storm and yours will be calmed.

Expect rewards. Rewards are gifts that come when the channel is cleared and emptied by giving of self to others. To keep the gifts coming, keep giving them away.

It's exciting to think the soul might guide us to someone who might be made better just by being around us. Yet that's exactly how Cayce tells us to live.

"When an entity or soul so lives, so manifests its ideals that others are not only attracted to, but desire in themselves to be better for having known—and having been with—such a body, then growth may be assured in the experience of any soul."

When you are living the principles of the secret self, expect change. Change requires decisions. The very process of allowing the secret self to have its life means there will be more choices, more decisions to make, than ever before. It does not mean everything automatically works out right. Life doesn't get any easier—just more exciting. If it isn't exciting, you're missing the boat.

You participate in the process by honing your sense of purpose to match the secret self's ideal. Then the two of you —your known self and your secret self—boldly walk through the doors that open. But what if more than one door opens at the same time? Let your secret self make the decision.

Whenever you have a decision to make, go back to the three questions. Ask your soul to tell you what, why, and how. Write your answers from the space between breathing in and breathing out. In meditation, ask your soul what it would have you do and know.

Your soul wants to surrender to God's soul. Allow it by consciously willing your soul to surrender. Say, "My soul surrenders to the soul of my Creator, which is the Spirit that gives me life." Then watch out.

That surrender activates every universal law in the universe. But don't let that frighten you. The individual law of attraction will draw, as though by some mysterious force, people, places, things, circumstances, and situations that will appeal in a negative or positive way. Stuff just *shows up*, and it's all to help you make that decision. You see, the soul living its mission isn't alone. The Creator desires more than anything for you to make it. After a while you may begin to believe Music is writing songs just for you because you need to hear the words. *And it is!*

Living this process suddenly means the universe exists for your benefit. And you for its. If that thought terrifies you too much to walk boldly through the doors that open, then crawl. But go. Your soul is headed home and taking you with it. Are you going to say no to *that?*

Soul guidance also comes through dreams. If you're too busy to listen during the day, it will talk to you at night. You'll have to write down your dreams to learn what your soul is telling you. The language of the soul is *Dreamspeak*: symbols with personal relevance. Your soul remembers what the symbols mean, but you may have forgotten. Therefore, pay close attention to everything. To your soul, dreams are the universal law of self-preservation. Your soul may guide you to studies of archetypal symbols that stir memories of better times, better places. Pay attention.

But soul guidance is equally likely to come through a television program or a book as through dreams. When you're living the principles and the process is in motion, everything becomes one. The inner world and the outer world become one world. Yours. The Creator's love floods your world with light so that you can see your options. But the Creator won't make your decisions for you. That's your job. That's the plan. "This day I set before you life and death. Choose life." In all things, choose life. Say yes. *Yes!* to life. To your secret self's life.

How to Recognize the Secret Self

Soul guidance presents itself differently to each person. Some experience it through the emotions in meditation. But an altered state of consciousness is not prerequisite to guidance for yourself or others. An emerging sensitivity to your needs and the needs of others is the natural result of living the ideal.

The words *psychic* and *intuitive* are interchangeable throughout the Cayce readings.

You may feel hunches, intuitive nudging. Acting on these feelings is one way to begin to distinguish between true intuition and mere anxiety. The secret self may present itself as a feeling in a particular area of the body, such as in the head or chest area. Or it may come as a feeling during a particular time of day, such as first thing on arising in the morning. As guidance often is nonverbal, intuition may be expressed through the arts.

An urge to draw, paint, or dance could signal the awakening of the secret self. Being drawn to a particular type of music not previously enjoyed can be taken as the secret self's announcement of its presence.

Of course, the most common experience is hearing or sensing the still, small voice within. But even that isn't always infallible.

The key factor in recognizing the true secret self, as opposed to another element of mind, such as the subconscious, is whether the hunches, nudgings, intuitions, feelings, visions, and the like, are in harmony with the secret self's ideal. Explained in Chapter 17, "Secrets of Prophecy," is how the subconscious distorts images. The secret self does not express the desires of the subconscious, but its own. Its own desires are attuned to its ideal and purpose, which is always unselfish. Confusion means the subconscious may be blocking the path of the secret self.

Guidance from the secret self never precipitates judgments of people about whom you are picking up signals. The secret self never judges, only evaluates.

Finally, there is one certain way to recognize the presence of the secret self. It is unexplainable, deeply felt, inexpressible joy. The soul allowed to live its life is simply happy.

If, however, you *ignore* the soul's guidance, and continually deny the intuitive impressions, the soul becomes unhappy, and makes itself felt through inner turmoil and stress.

"Master, there are so many helpless, homeless, hopeless, and poor. Why don't you help them?"

"I do. Through you. I have no hands but yours."

3

Secrets of Abundance

The secret to getting is giving with gratitude.

Cayce understood that getting and giving go together like rivers and fish: one comes out of the other. He said to measure ourselves not by what we have, but by what we give.

There are two types of giving: expected and unexpected.

Giving because it's expected, such as obligatory holiday gifts; office charities, bridal and baby showers; client perks, etc., all may preserve social status, but do little to lift the spirit, and can, in fact, make us grumpy. We sometimes feel we never get back as good as we give, but we do it routinely because it's expected.

Traditional religious services request and sometimes *require* giving, but even tithes can be handed over matter-of-factly, as though we were paying the phone bill in the hope of keeping another line of communication open. There is little God in giving with a closed heart, such as shoving a quarter into the hand of a beggar because we're embarrassed not to.

But unexpected giving can be fun.

A friend had been saving coins in an old red velvet purse that she kept hidden in the back of a closet. Pretty soon the purse was so heavy the strap would break if she tried to lift it. So at Christmastime she hauled the purse out of the closet, put it into a satchel with sturdy handles, and set out to locate a Salvation Army kettle, where she thoroughly startled the bell ringer by dumping several pounds of change into the black kettle. She threw the red velvet purse in to boot. The bell ringer said she'd never seen so many dimes, nickels, and quarters at one time in her life. The woman said she enjoyed the feeling of "pouring out a blessing."

Unexpected gifts for no reason except that someone cares are the nicest to receive, and therefore, the nicest to give. My friend surprised the bell ringer by the manner and method of the gift, but after all, it was Christmas, and the bell ringer's purpose was to attract the spirit of giving. So the next time this friend had a purse full of change, she looked for someone who did not appear either to be asking or needy. She spent the coins on a gift for a former teacher. She spent all day selecting the gift, all the while thinking loving thoughts of this mentor. The gift of time and thought, coupled with the few dollars, multiplied in her mind tenfold so that by the time she presented the gift, she truly had received more joy than she was giving.

Abundance is a two-step process:

1. Giving and saying thank you.
2. Receiving and saying thank you.

Giving with gratitude for the opportunity to give is the universal law of love. It applies to giving money, time, energy, effort, encouragement, support, patience, hope, and kindness. It applies twenty-four hours a day to every living creature and thing on the planet. Universal laws are immutable and irrefutable regardless of century or society, unchangeable by kings or fashion. They have governed since the beginning, and will govern until the end as we know it.

Another law governing abundance, as well as the law of love, is the universal law of cause and effect. This one is known by many names: the law of reciprocity, the law of the tenfold return, the law of stewardship, the law of recompense, and so forth. Some even call it the universal law of karma. It simply means that for every action there is a direct reaction. There is a relationship between actions or events in that one or more are always the result of the other or others.

In other words, *as ye sow, ye reap*. When you give with gratitude to the universe, the universe gives back—in spades, with interest, multiplied.

"Try me," God says. "See if I won't fill your barns and storehouses to overflowing."

Try it. You can't outgive God.

Try an experiment. Pinpoint a need. Say, for example, that in your work you feel cheated, underpaid, and unappreciated. You've been doing the work of three people, arriving early and staying late, but nobody seems to notice. The expended time, energy, and effort isn't paying off and you resent it.

Tomorrow morning while dressing for work, talk to your concept of God. (If you haven't got one, get one, or it's all for naught.) Thank your God for this job, and for the opportunity to give everything you've got to it. Thank God for your boss, your co-workers—especially the one you dislike most. Thank God for your meager wages.

Go through the motions even if you don't mean it, but try to muster up a thimbleful of sincerity. It isn't all that tough when you remember the homeless. They serve to remind you that any job is better than no job.

Throughout the day, give that job everything you've got and say thank you. Say it to yourself, to God, and everyone you meet. Put up a sign in big red letters: THANK YOU. In effect, shout it to the universe. No matter what happens, say thank you—I mean, *no matter what*.

Repeat this for forty days. I guarantee, if followed without fail, something will be different at the end of the forty days. It could be the job that will be different, or it could be *you*. But you'll never again doubt the power and magic of those two little words.[1]

There's another universal law weaving throughout this process of saying thank you for forty days. It's the law of like begets like. That means we "father" that which is like us. We procreate, generate, and cause all the good that is happening to us—as well as that perceived as "bad."

This method of giving with gratitude shifts the focus away from a consciousness of lack to a consciousness of plenty. This evokes the universal law of expectancy. Some degree of what we look forward to or regard as likely to happen eventually happens. If you want plenty, act as though you already have it.

Failure to follow this basic principle can lead to disaster.

Dick and Jayne owned a nice little $1 million per year business that netted them personally, before taxes, around $120,000. Life was sweet. There was a snazzy little roadster convertible, a diamond here and there, a trip or two each year, plus goodies whenever the notion struck. They were generous with themselves and their friends, and though they didn't tithe regularly, Jayne would write a fat check to some charity or other fairly often.

Economic hardship hit the community, and almost every small business was affected, including Dick and Jayne's. They panicked. Instead of saying thank you and holding a consciousness of plenty, cutbacks ensued immediately. Decisions had to be made quickly. Employees had to bite the bullet and forgo raises. The trips stopped. A consciousness of lack pervaded the atmosphere. The creditors started calling. They had to be paid. The charities called for their contributions. They didn't have to be made. All "unnecessary" spending stopped. Dick and Jayne forgot the first rule of prosperity: Give and say thank you.

Their crippled company was years recovering before Dick

[1] I gratefully acknowledge my debt to Everett Irion for introducing the concept of saying *thank you* no matter what, and for drumming it into my head until I finally believed him.

and Jayne woke up and recognized their mistakes—one of stewardship, another of unbelief in God's laws. But they fared better than some, particularly Evan.

Evan's company grossed $10 million a year. His reputation as a wheeler-dealer was legendary. It seemed he was on a power trip without end. He barely missed the half of the business his wife took in the divorce. The children chose to live with him, and the house was filled with good times and laughter. He forgot the law of cause and effect and became a master of self-aggrandizement, buying entire restaurants for an evening to impress his friends. Unlike Dick and Jayne, Evan didn't cut back on anything when hard times hit—not the parties, not the toy buying, not the alcohol. Today, he is committed to a mental hospital, declared incompetent by the courts to manage his own affairs.

The lesson from Dick and Jayne and Evan is, or course, that misuse of resources, coupled with lack of faith and a maniacal ego involvement with money, inevitably results in unnecessary losses. The Bible teaches that all the money in the entire world belongs to God, and if we find ourselves in control of some of it, we must recognize that a projection of spirit into earth—called green energy—has been placed into our care. The responsibility of managing money plays right into the commandment to love one another. It's a commandment that cannot be broken without eventual consequences.

Often it appears that the most unworthy among us acquire the greatest riches, and, Cayce said, that what might be "counted to some as sin or error may in reality be mercy to that soul from an all-wise, beneficent Father, who is directing, planning, giving the soul an opportunity for the use of that which may come into the soul's experience in the material plane. What the soul . . . does about the knowledge . . . is the opportunity for that soul to develop."

How to share our resources is a personal decision, made within the framework of our own awareness. The questions of giving, how much, when, and to whom are private, and best, like prayer, remain secreted from the secular world. But we are told to think on those things that help us answer

the question, "Am I my brother's keeper?"[2] As our souls
develop, we become more aware of our duty to others.

Some truly wealthy people have understood this duty.
Billions of dollars are circulated by the fabulously rich
yearly, some of it in the form of seed money.[3]

Stories of the rich and famous and how they got that way
abound in the business world. Hard work and dedication
are usually the main ingredients touted as necessary for
guaranteed success. But in *Seed Money in Action*, Jon
Speller quotes John D. Rockefeller, Jr. as having said, "I
have been brought up to believe, and the conviction only
grows upon me, that giving ought to be entered into in just
the same careful way as investing."

While we may lack the financial savvy to enter into
giving—or investing—with care, we need not fear making
a mistake if we remember that Cayce said not to count any
good act lost. In other words, don't worry about whether
you're giving to the needy or the greedy. No seed falls to
the ground without the Father's knowledge.

Speller writes: "Andrew Carnegie, Julius Rosenwald, and
Andrew Mellon all knew the Law of Seed Money and
practiced it throughout long and extremely prosperous lives.
Not only did the gifts of these men enrich the entire world,
but they also multiplied their personal wealth, because each
of them knew how to claim their multiplied return of his
gifts and constantly did so claim."

Speller calls money in circulation "God in action." As
God is love, there is as much love in the activities of those
doing their best with the talents entrusted to them as in the
smile of a babe or the beauty of a song. By doing our best
with what we have, we build into ourselves an awareness of
plenty.

An editor with whom I've worked, Janice Hall, holds this
consciousness of plenty so close to the surface of her being

---

[2]Genesis 4:9.
[3]*Seed Money in Action,* by Jon P. Speller.

that it's visible. Her material needs are met apparently through doing a job she loves. However, it's her abundant willingness to give of her sense of self-worth that attracts writers, often the lowliest of the downtrodden. She exudes an attitude that says: "If you need a cheerful word, come to me. I have plenty. If you need more time, come to me. I have plenty. If you need someone to take an interest in you, come to me. I have plenty."

After observing her for years, always pleasant, always smiling, finally I asked her how she became so stable and content. Surprised, she answered, "Oh, I don't know. I was just always told I was the perfect child of God, and that I could do no wrong." Parents, pay attention.

Clearly she's doing the best she can with the talents given her, and apparently is given more in return. Her writers are devoted to her and give her the best of themselves. She sows seeds of encouragement and harvests writing worth publishing.

As Janice Hall holds up the star for her writers, we can hold up the star for someone else. Often, supporting another's illusions is just another way of helping their dreams come true.

The Bible teaches us that to sow tiny little seeds is to get back not only more seeds to sow, but to harvest the life contained in the seeds. As the oak's secrets reside inside the acorn, so God's secret gifts reside inside our thoughts. We can't see the oak by analyzing the acorn, even under a four-story-high microscope, but we know the oak is in there. Does the acorn know? Would it withhold its gift if it knew?

When we withhold kindness and gentleness from another, we are asking for a harvest of a harsh, lonely existence.

The pervading notion of today's pop psychology that we have to give to ourselves that which we need is like eating the seeds instead of the harvest. We are constantly told to give ourselves "strokes," to put ourselves first, to love ourselves more. *More than whom?* It takes two to make a back rub—one to give and one to receive. When two are unselfish, they trade places. The problem seems to come when one does all the giving and one all the getting.

Cayce gave a reading for a fellow who thought the idea of giving only applied to mediocre minds, or to people of certain faiths, but not to him. Cayce said the same rules apply to shoestring vendors and bank presidents alike. Apparently, the fellow had been boasting about how generous he would be if only he had a lot of money. Cayce told him that since he didn't give from his meager lot, he would possibly be even stingier if he had millions. And harder to get along with.

Cayce said what we give to others we give to God, but that we really can't give anything to God because it all belongs to God anyway. But when we say *thanks* to others for the opportunity to give, we're saying it to God. Our own needs go unmet until we focus the spiritual magnifier on the needs of others and begin to give as we have.

If we don't have it, we can't give it. But Cayce said to ask what we would do with it if we had it.

An ill woman, seeking abundant health, was told to figure out why she wanted to be healthy and she would be. The profound truth behind that idea almost escapes detection until it's transferred to areas concerning money, energy, and time.

Without giving any real thought to why we want them, we complain about lack of money, energy, and time. Feeling needy in these areas and griping about it is a popular pastime. A question worth asking is, *What would we do with them if we had more of them?* Would we spend them with gratitude in some type of service to others?

The same question applies to our need for love, encouragement, support, patience, hope, and kindness. If we had more of them in our lives, would we give them to others?

Then the magic phrase, *thank you,* is the way to get them. Take hope, for example.

It may sound strange at first, but try as an experiment saying, "Thank you, God, for the lack of hope in my life."

Immediately the truly hopeless come to mind. By feeling hopeless you *feel for* the hopeless because you *know* how it feels. If you know from firsthand experience the painful emptiness, that black, endless chasm that marks the end of the line—God, how it *hurts*—you may spend the rest of your life making sure no one ever has to feel that alone. If you've been there you can help them in a way no one else can. You can give as you have received. By giving hope to others, you get your own.

Giving energy with gratitude short-circuits burnout. Cayce warned against giving to gain a hold that we can use in an underhanded manner, but said if giving service, then *spend it all*. He said if we run out of energy, it isn't because we stopped asking for it, it's because we stopped giving. Or we let self-pity over lack of appreciation creep in. Abundant energy is ours when we are fed by the joy of giving.

If you really get caught up in the joy of giving, it's easy to forget to say thank you for the gifts. But receiving and saying thank you is step two of the secret of abundance.

In fact, often we don't recognize a gift when it's handed to us. Generally, that's because what we receive is so much bigger than what we gave, that we fail to make the connection. That mistake, when discovered, can make you feel like an ungrateful wretch. You see, these universal laws that govern abundance don't care whether we understand them. They work anyway. As I discovered.

A letter arrived requesting a five-dollar donation. It happened to be for a cause with personal relevance, so I sent fifty dollars and forgot about it. A couple of days later the phone rang. An editor offered to pay my expenses to cover an event. I hemmed and hawed and said I'd have to let him know at 9:30 the next morning. I decided other commitments were pressing, and I'd have to say no. At 9:29 the following morning, the phone rang. It was my mother. I explained about the offer and told her I'd decided to decline. She, in effect, told me I was nuts, to drop everything and go. I did.

At some point later it dawned on me that I'd given ten

times what was asked for in the letter and received $500 worth of freebies, exactly ten times what I'd given. I felt so stupid for almost saying no to this obvious universal gift, I decided to stop saying no and start saying *yes, thank you* to everything, a method I can personally recommend.

Another secret to abundance with which I've had personal experience is a technique called *Designing the Ideal Day*.

This technique was first described to me by Edgar Cayce's grandson, Charles Thomas Cayce, during a course titled *Exploring the Mysteries of Your Mind*.

Charles Thomas had described how he had culled this idea, based on "mind is the builder," from his grandfather's readings. After he had embraced the life, meaning he was more or less living the principles described in the previous chapter, he realized a valid experiment would be to design an ideal day sometime in the future to see what would happen. He approached the experiment as a test of the information in the readings to determine for himself whether mind truly is the builder.

He wrote on a piece of paper what he considered to be an ideal day some seven years in the future. He outlined his day, starting with morning chores on a farm which he would own, and even specified the type of vehicle he would drive to the various activities throughout this ideal day. Then he put the piece of paper away, and as far as he can recall, did not look at it again for seven years.

One morning seven years later, upon waking, his eyes fell on the book where he had placed the paper. As he read what he'd written, he realized the day he was about to live was eerily close to the one he'd planned.

After hearing Charles Thomas speak so reverently of his experience, I decided to try it for myself.

I designed three ideal days for the future. The first would happen in three days. It was general, and related to a specific question I hoped to have answered. It didn't happen— my question wasn't answered then, but later.

The second ideal day I planned for three weeks away. I really stretched and said that I would awaken ready to pack for a trip there was absolutely no foreseeable way I could afford. I try, but don't always remember, to live by "if money can fix it, it ain't a problem." But I'd said the money would miraculously appear, and it did. Not every specific detail I'd outlined concerning the trip happened, but vaguely related events did occur.

The third ideal day I planned was for three years in the future. At this writing the time has not passed, so I can't report the results.

But this clearly demonstrates how mind builds through the governing universal law of expectancy.

Too, an element of the universal law of attraction activates when we approach life in this way. Of course, holding thoughts of poverty and lack attracts poverty and lack. In physics, the law of attraction is the electric or magnetic force that acts between oppositely charged bodies, tending to draw them together. In spiritual development, we may keep attracting the same conditions again and again until we have neutralized the magnetic field by finally learning the lesson the condition would teach us.

The mental powers can easily be misused. I know personally of one man on welfare who keeps himself alive by visualizing finding purses. *He finds them!* Often. Then he grinds his teeth at night in guilt over not returning the ones that contain owner identification. I asked him why he didn't use his exceptional visualization powers to find a *job*. He simply said, "Jobs and I don't get along." Bless him, and so be it, but Lord, what he could do if he'd expend that energy honestly, "finding" enough money to fund, for example, a research project. He epitomizes the servant who misused his talent.

If we misuse our powers for self, the law of cause and effect will take us down—eventually. But if we use them "aright," as Cayce said, the same law will take us anywhere we need to be to fulfill our purpose for being born—and will pick up the tab.

Before designing your ideal day, read Chapter 7, "Secrets of the Little Choo Choo." And note that the principles in Chapter 2 were in place in Charles Thomas's life before he worked with the experiment, and at least somewhat, in mine, too.

> "Master, why must they suffer so? Must they always?"
> "Only until you learn what they are here to teach you."

4

Secrets of Loving
and Being Loved

The secret to loving is to love. The secret to being loved is to be lovable. We don't like to hear that because it puts the responsibility for not being loved enough on our shoulders—where it belongs. Fortunately, the universal of grace and mercy governs the best love relationships. Grace is immunity and unmerited favor. Mercy is a reprieve from a fate of considerable severity without further implication. The law of grace and mercy, then, is *another chance*.

Cayce said if we expect love, we should make ourselves lovable. Who among us is so lovable we never need another chance?

If you are half of a significant love relationship, or

marriage, what did you say, feel, and do when you got up this morning and looked at the one you're with?

Did you speak? Were you polite? Was it in the same way you would be to a co-worker or a stranger on the street?

Did you touch? And apologize for getting in each other's way?

Did you feel connected? Or did you feel shackled or imprisoned, or even lonely?

Questers for secrets of the universe are generally channels of Spirit—caring, gentle souls, lovers of creation, children of the one true God. But when it comes to relationships, we're about as dumb as the next person.

Cayce said if we don't love our worst enemy, we haven't even begun to develop. Yet often we act as though our worst enemy is living under the same roof. We're pillowing with, sharing meals with, and trying to build a life with someone we can't—or don't—even talk to; and many of us have been at it for thirty or forty years. What makes us different from the next person is that we accept, as truth, that when there is any sort of lack in our lives, it's our doing. We don't resignedly accept what comes and shrug as if those were the breaks. If we're being honest, we know we set it up. We're reaping the harvest of seeds sown. But there's more to it.

We are *required* to see the spiritual essence, "that which you would *worship*" in a person—even our mate. That does not mean to miss the humanness, but to integrate the two.

Author Harmon Bro tells of trying to come to grips with this startling concept:

"When I first heard Cayce's astonishing saying, I was sitting in his sunny study (during a reading), while he spoke quietly in trance from the studio couch across the room. Was the poised and measured voice only using poetic extravagance to make a point? Must we really see in each person that which we worship? Probably Cayce's saying directed us to affirm the soul origin and divine spark of each person we took on, right while we bought groceries from them, or chatted with them on the phone, or gave orders to an employee.

"This approach didn't get me very far. I split my attention trying to perceive each time an essence, an origin, a spiritual core. As a result I missed some of the direct impact of a freckle-faced grin, a sexy walk, a child's babble. Trying to think about ultimate spiritual substances took me away from real encounters, so that while I felt vaguely elevated, I wasn't all there in my seeing. Certainly I would have missed some of the earthy humanity of the Master had I met Him on a rocky country road in Galilee long ago and looked only for the divine principle incarnated in Him.

"But I managed in time to stop my nibbling, chattering, slot-using, analyzing, consuming mind for an instant while I was simply present with another person, as all of that individual's knobby uniqueness shone upon me. A phrase from the Christian mystics helped—a kind of prayer called 'simple regard,' meaning undivided and unprocessed, wordless direct attention to God. So I set about practicing simple regard for people I met on my daily rounds."

After Bro told this story, one night at a small-group meeting, an elderly gentleman speaking of his marriage of forty-one years said, "It's probably a case of two people who should have never married. But, of course, it's too late to do anything about it now... about forty tragic years too late."

Bro's story of learning simple regard pierced my awareness as being the missing element in this man's and many other relationships. I wanted to cry, "Didn't you ever once just appreciate one another's own knobby uniqueness?"

How sad that we miss the impact we could have on one another if we'd just *be together and shine on one another.* An occasional few moments of undivided and unprocessed, wordless direct attention to each other in real encounters, where we're really all there in our seeing, worshipful moments, with no nibbling, chattering, slotting, or analyzing allowed. Such moments of selfless giving would be better than, as Erma Bombeck puts it, "a whole lifetime of Godiva chocolates and Hallmark cards."

Is it ever too late to wake up and give?

Not every relationship has to include sexual love, but life is about spiritual love, and while God is love, love is giving, even if it's only simple regard. If there's any truth in "as ye sow, ye reap," then awakening each morning and asking, "What can I give my mate today?" is the secret key to the kingdom of heaven. Cayce called giving "the passkey to the throne."

If some of this sounds similar to the chapter on "Secrets of Abundance," it's because it is. Abundant love comes to us when we give it with gratitude. Often in our attempts to do what is *expected* of each other—and only the shadow knows what *that* is nowadays—we wind up making deals over whose turn it is to put out the cat. When schedule conflicts prevent one from keeping the bargain, we keep score and respond unkindly to the other's perceived neglect of little things. These conflicts may escalate into open wounds, gulfs of disappointment and anger that must be crossed if we are to come back to the center together.

What greater gift to present to the other than unexpected kindness, gentleness, and patience. And simple regard. The Father made us love because like begets like. A loving Giver created us. How can we be less?

Beyond Equality

Edgar Cayce's most famous tenet is, "Mind is the builder and Spirit is the Life." Genesis infers that Mind the Builder is *masculine,* and Spirit the Life is *feminine*. Herein lies the secret to ending the battle between the sexes.

The most loving women, spiritual-type females, feel particularly distressed by the battle, yet have a particular problem: the shortage of spiritual-type males to love—men who can embrace their feminine natures. It isn't enough that a man is a loving, monogamous heterosexual who earns his share of the living. We want a mate who is conversant in the ethereal realm.

When women urge men to express the feminine, we don't expect of them painted fingernails and lace dresses, but we've been unable to articulate just what we do mean. We speak of preferring men who are gently sensitive, but that often gets translated into womanly, therefore, *unmanly* and *weak*.

That isn't what we want. What we do want is a mate with whom to form a co-creative pairbonding.

Finding one man who fulfills all our expectations is not impossible, but it is difficult. The inner world has been primarily a woman's domain. We little girls were encouraged to actualize our dreams and to develop such "feminine" virtues as intuition, nurturing, serving others, and the ability to surrender. We look for a man worth surrendering to and expect him to exhibit strength, ambition, dependability, and to gain power and material sufficiency.

Little boys were encouraged to risk life and limb outwardly—athletically on the playing field, corporately in the board room—but not to claim their feminine side. When they risk venturing inward, as male novices of the inner life, often they find it necessary to shake off the trappings of the outer world and stalk Truth as they once stalked wild game—for survival. Often their love relationships suffer, to say nothing of their work lives.

For men and women alike, unifying purpose and profession into one gloriously cohesive life usually requires self-interrogation. Women generally are less resistant to this inner-discovery process, hence church and inner-journey organizations usually contain more women than men. Men and women alike need role models for loving and being loved.

For men—both the old-style traditional and the enlightened—a role model for embracing their feminine nature is Mary's Joseph of the New Testament.

Joseph was not weak or unmanly, self-centered or egotistical. He was a loving, caring, giving man, sensitive, intuitive, and obedient unto God, who spoke to him through dreams. He validated and supported Mary's mission, and devoted himself to being her caretaker. Suppose he hadn't?

Suppose upon learning of Mary's pregnancy he had not accepted the role of servant to the new creation; had not transcended Jewish tradition, which demanded she be put away privately? Suppose he had ignored his dream and had not recognized through his angelic, intuitive faculties that something was alive and growing in Mary that would change the world? Suppose he had not subdued his ego, laid aside his fears of public opinion, and nurtured mother and child as needed? What he would have missed!

Mary and Joseph are perfect examples of co-creative pairbonding, with Joseph expressing Spirit and Mary expressing Mind.

Women today still often think that expressing the masculine and using our minds means competing in a "man's world." We don flannel pinstripes in an attempt to blur gender identity, spiritually asexualizing ourselves. We are confusing male and female with masculine and feminine. They are not one and the same. Women—both oppressed and liberated—also need a role model for embracing their masculine nature. Such is Mary.

Mary was not aggressive or angry, but submissive—*to God, not to Joseph*.

She knew herself to be valuable. After conceiving, she spoke powerfully of her vision of herself as blessed and the great things God was doing through her. Speechmaking is a product of Mind. Joseph's role was to keep and protect Mary and to bring her conception safely to life. Protective service is a product of Spirit. Even one so favored as Mary needed a male, human partner to help her with her mission, indicating that *all* light bearers need help.

Nowadays women, *still* trying to shatter oppressing traditions—including the one of always supporting *his* work at the expense of hers—are winding up as utterly disgusted, confused, and angry females who feel the need to assert. Relationships with men who feel threatened—who won't, by God, be trampled into submission—are vaporizing in the battle heat. That's not how it was meant to be. Look again at Genesis.

Genesis indicates Mind is masculine and Spirit is feminine, and both exist in all creation, not only the plant and animal kingdoms, regardless which gender embodies. "Mind is the builder and Spirit is the life" is demonstrated in Genesis when the Creator's own feminine Spirit moved, giving life to the Universal Mind's creation, which was, until then, "without form and void." The Hebrew word is *tohuw*: "worthless." Nothing comes to life until Spirit moves.

Luke 1:38 shows Mary subjugating her conscious mind to the Father's when she said, "Be it unto me according to Thy word." Then the Holy Spirit, moving on the Father's Mind—which, according to the Cayce readings, extends beyond brain center functions, throughout the whole body—caused Mary to conceive. It was Genesis repeated. The Father spoke, Spirit moved, and Light came into the world. Mary became a vessel of creation, just as the Universe became the vessel of creation in the beginning.

Men and women alike can be or become vessels of creation, and it is probable that in co-creative pairbonding each person embodies traits of both Mary and Joseph, and each half of the couple trades off roles as necessary.

Being chromosomally endowed with certain instincts does not negate the fact that in both sexes, masculine thrusts forth images, such as when artist Georgia O'Keeffe thrust forth images animated by Spirit onto canvas.

In each of us Spirit serves by giving life to what mind creates, be it a child, a book, a painting, or a career. When two people join minds and spirits in serving one another's creations, arguments stimulated by traditional role-playing vaporize in the sense of wonderment and joy. Our task is to get a sense of our own as well as the other's mission, whatever that might be; to find something to support and nurture in one another. Mind needs Spirit to give life, but Spirit needs Mind in order to have something to give life to.

Joseph knew Mary's task before he married her. Traditionally, we marry before getting a sense of what our work is to be. Then, when one discovers it and the other hasn't, the other begins to feel neglected and leaves—or wants to.

In loving, we must somehow comprehend this: As androgynous souls possessing both male and female, as well as both masculine and feminine characteristics, we were fathered by Mind and mothered by Spirit and given the Universal Mind with which to create. Some of us became chaotic miscreants, necessitating a human mind, which blocked the consciousness of the Universal Mind, with which we've been trying to reconnect ever since. Our souls implore the effort, though futile if we fail to connect with the integrity in one another.

As lovers, we require the courage of a Mary and a Joseph, in ourselves and in a partner, to surrender to and integrate both the masculine and the feminine natures and to recognize each other as co-creative servants *of one another.*

This goes beyond equality. Of course, it is an error to believe the Creator intended there be a dominant sex or color. But merely being equal is insufficient. Perhaps when the battle ends we will lighten up on one another, and rise from the ashes, as Edgar Cayce said, "equal to being in our Creator's presence."

General Advice from the Readings

Edgar Cayce held contemporary views on relationships. Media bombards us with "how to communicate" articles, books, and television programs. Studies reveal we divorce most often for lack of emotional intimacy. The advice given in the readings on the secret of how to sustain a relationship is startlingly relevant to the advent of the twenty-first century.

• A thirty-year-old woman asked Cayce how to make her husband fall in love with her again, and why she and her husband had so little in common, so little to talk about. He told her that she was meeting herself from the previous sojourn, when she and her husband were father and daughter. Apparently, they each brought to the relationship an inability to communicate, caused by a need to be separate individuals. Cayce told her to study her inner self first, to determine what was motivating her, and to decide what, for her, would be the ideal home. He told her not to be concerned with what her husband or anyone else might consider as ideal, but to decide for herself what *she* wanted, then do what her spiritual self told her to do. Cayce said that she had to choose for herself, and her husband had to choose for himself, just how they wanted this thing to work out. He told her she might have to separate from her husband unless he had surgery for a physical condition that prevented him from desiring a physical relationship with her. Only he could choose to change that.

Cayce gave the young woman the secret to relationships when he, in effect, said not to be concerned with what was, but to study within self first, and to decide how *she wants it to be now*. He told another couple, however, that it would destroy both of them if they separated.

• Cayce gave a joint reading to a husband and wife, whom he told that whenever either of them was in turmoil, neither should do all the praying or all the cussing alone, but together "they must ask." He indicated they were together this time to learn to cooperate and to coordinate their efforts through bearing a child. He said that nothing else would bring them the understanding and comprehension of what each of their abilities could accomplish. He said that each of them would become better, that their love, respect, faith, and confidence in each other would expand.

• Prior to an impending marriage, someone (it isn't clear who was doing the asking) inquired of Cayce whether a young couple were suited to one another. The inquirer was told that for the moment, the couple's minds, bodies, and desires were in harmony, but that trouble might strike. Cayce said, though, that they could use turmoil, dissensions, and strife as stepping stones to greater opportunities and privileges as helpmates to one another if they didn't become self-centered and allow selfish motives to make demands on one another. If selfishness caused them to satisfy their desires without regard for the other, it would cause division between them.

He said they loved each other now, but that love is giving and growth. It may be cultivated or it may be scared. When we give because we are scared not to, it isn't really love. One person cannot sit still and expect the other to do all the giving or forgiving. They have to try to complement each other.

The couple could be happy and compatible if they realized that happiness and compatibility are *made*. Cayce said such a state doesn't just exist, and that their union would be more worthwhile if they learned interdependency; that each had to be able to depend on the other; that the changes life would bring would have to be met together if they were to be happy.

He said they should be on equal footing with one another; that each should take an interest in the activities of the other; that they should meet one another on their own respective ground. To accomplish this, Cayce said, they should study one another—not each other's whims and fancies, but how to bring out the best in each other. He said not to study for the purpose of being critical of one another, but to complement each other; that each should have his own job; to leave the office at the office when at home; to leave the petty things of home at home when abroad.

Cayce said their sex life should be kept inviolate, and that no one (perhaps the inquirer) should try to influence whether they should have children; that this should be left to the "Giver of those opportunities."

• A man who asked what effect a marriage to a particular woman would have on his life was asked what effect he wanted it to have; that it would become whatever he allowed it to become; that it depended on his choices. Cayce seemed to be warning the man that he might be as sorry as God was when he said, "I repent that I ever made man." The man was reminded that men and women are free-willed, and if we *choose* correctly, the result is contentment, happiness, and joy. But if our choices are made for the purpose of self-glorification, the result is inharmony, mistrust, turmoil, and strife. Universal law has declared it so. He was told the marriage had been blocked each time it had been planned because of resentments he was holding.

• A woman wanted to know why she was with her husband, and how they could accomplish what they were supposed to do together. She also expressed concern over his lack of financial generosity. Cayce told her to be just as generous to her husband as she expected him to be with her. He reminded her that everything starts in the mind; that physical results depend on how the mind is guided by the spirit.

As for how to accomplish their mission: *By each being true to themselves*. Cayce said they were together because of attractions born in other "activities."

Relationships Are Risky Business to the Soul

We each bring into relationships the combined results of our heredity, environmental influences, and the thought patterns that have made us what we are. We seek someone who can accept the whole of us, especially the soul of us.

No matter who we are, we need someone we trust enough to let them see us at our worst—and best. It seems strange that we should withhold the best of ourselves from the one we love, but it happens out of fear that should they reject or scorn the deepest, most spiritual side of us, the pain would be too great to bear.

We sometimes expect rejection when we're ill-tempered; we even hope for it so we can learn from it. If the facade we show the world is rejected, what does it matter, as it isn't really us anyway. It's easy to change our clothes and hairstyle and try again. But should someone get close enough to come in contact with our soul, then reject *that*, it would be devastating. So we keep that part hidden away, we think—safe, out of sight, out of mind.

But the stirring soul will not stay quiet; it must express itself, for that is why it came into the earth. It will not be denied forever. And so we move from lover to lover, looking for the one whom we dare stand truly naked before, the very essence of us bared.

Continual risk, exposure to the chance of injury or loss, marks the developing relationship as each one dares to grow and change. Without it, the relationship becomes stagnant, like a dead sea, where nothing can live.

We who find ourselves drowning in a dead-sea relationship can heed Cayce's reminder that we did not come into materiality or into the relationship on a whim, but through our own choice, through channels open to us. A relationship—especially a marriage—is a workshop for the soul. Therefore, even this association can be used as an opportunity to know God better. We are to use such opportunities, not abuse them; keep the body, the mind, the whole of the intent and purpose circumspect.

As for what to do about it, we are to listen to *conscience* in prayer and meditation for what it will tell us; and remember, "My Spirit beareth witness with thy Spirit. This is the answer then to each soul."

5

Secrets of
Family Relationships

The secret of family relationships is that we are our own heirs.

But did you ever think you were born into the wrong body? What am I doing in this thing? Its eyes are weak. Its ears hear only what they want to. Its joints creak and hurt. It's lazy. Sometimes its brain fails me completely—it gets all discombobulated when I really get going, and it doesn't take much to confuse it. Plus, it has the metabolism of a hibernating bear.

Now Cayce tells me it's the body I needed for soul development—the right body and the right family.

Did you ever think you were born into the wrong family? Not according to Cayce. Your birth family was selected precisely for the opportunities for soul development it would provide. *Selected by whom?* Is there some group of ancient entities acting as karmic travel agents, booking reservations into this family or that? According to Cayce, soul development is the *only* reason we are *allowed* to be born.

The family is a group with its own vibration, composed of the vibrations of each member, living and dead. We seek a vibration harmonious with our own so that influences may be made known. Read the chapter titled "Secrets of the Soul's World" to understand "influences"; they have to do with moving through the borderlands, which seems to be in the Cayce readings the domain of the soul. In knowing—whatever there is to know—we meet and conquer self, which is separated from the Creator.

The vibrations, influences, and activities that surrounded our parents throughout the gestation period called for your soul and mine—and we answered. Otherwise we wouldn't be here.

The entering soul has no influence on the mother building the body. (Well, that's better. I'd hate to think I actually *created* this thing.) Flesh and blood is built by flesh and blood. Soul consists of what has been built through mind. However, your physical body is the one your soul needed for its development. Through your body, your soul expresses.

What about mind?

Your past is inherited each time you are reborn. With each incarnation, you get a new flesh and blood body and a new physical mind, but the soul mind is the same old set of sails. Mind is the shipbuilder—not of flesh and blood, but of the ship of the soul, the soul body. The soul mind builds the soul body with stuff dreams are made of: images, impressions, memories, and their associated vibrations. In a new human being, the new physical mind processes information about the new environment, but the reactions to that information come from the soul mind.

This set of sails has seen every blow, remembers every rip and tear from every tempest in the sea. Some kids come in like old seafarers. They've got *experience*. You can't tell them anything. Others have learned from the storms and are eager to hear of others' experiences and to share theirs. Still others don't want to be here at all, but at the soul level, know they must be.

Parenting is—or should be—seen as a privilege.

The attitude of the parents determines the nature of the soul attracted, the child born. Would-be parents who question the wisdom of bringing a child into such a world as the one we live in today should recognize the self-doubt being created by asking the question. The question cannot be answered except within the hearts and minds of those asking.

The command, "Be thou fruitful and multiply," sets in motion natural mental and spiritual laws according to whether the purpose for bearing a child would gratify flesh or would complete the relationship to the Creator. Souls that come as our children are lent to us by the Creator. How we treat that child, and the purposes we impress on that child, we send back to the Maker in the end.

How can we as parents attract a "good" child?

Don't even try.

The ultimate attempt to control another is to attempt to influence the soul being attracted by thinking certain thoughts. A prospective mother should prepare herself mentally and physically, knowing that, spiritually, *how she treats others* determines the nature and manner of the soul being attracted.

But others, not only the mother, are involved in attracting the soul.

The physical development of the child is wholly dependent upon the mother from whom it draws physical sustenance, but its purposes, desires, and hopes, are built up or influenced by the minds of *all* concerned, including the father and other relatives. Or maybe even the townspeople or the city, state, or town itself.

Did you ever wonder why you were born where you were? Did you feel like a foreigner in a strange land? Was it destiny? Or did it seem so?

The first environment of a particular sojourn through earth is inherited. It more or less comes with the territory of the parental vibrations. However, each country, state, city, or town has its own vibration, a blend created by all the people who live there. These vibrations create an attraction for the soul to the region. Also, climates and weather patterns, as well as opportunities for creative expression, carry associated vibrations that make an impression in the area we identify as being between time and space. Incoming souls may feel these vibrations, which are harmonious with their own, and may be attracted to a particular region because of them.

Cayce told a thirteen-year-old boy that he had been attracted into earth because of the activities the environment would provide. Then he was warned not to abuse this opportunity self-indulgently. But Cayce insisted that "Sing Sing, Hartford, or Timbuktu, the Lord is God of the Universe," and the Nazarene was born in a stable.

So what's our problem? Is it heredity or is it environment?

Take habits (all my bad ones; take them—please). Habits are akin to desire and not necessarily inherited. Habits are an environmental reaction of the senses, sparked by desire. Desire originates at three levels: mental, spiritual, and physical.

Or delinquency, inherited only in that a child "inherits" the environment its parents have created, or that certain familial vibratory patterns attract the incoming soul. Delinquency is caused more by community environment, which includes practically the whole world since TV has made it seem as though we live in one global community. Cayce said fifty years ago that juvenile delinquency is caused by "delinquency in high places." What would he say today?

Cayce held futuristic views on raising children. He viewed the birth of a child as the advent of a soul into the earth for the purpose of experiencing his or her true relationship with God. But one gets the feeling he wouldn't have favored MTV.

Children should be taught, he said, to recognize the defamation of the relationship between men and women as we observe it through media, books, song, and "movements of the body in the entertainments." And this was fifty years ago!

About sex education, he said not to wait for adolescence. During the first nine or ten years, children should be taught the beauty and sacredness of sex. He said to teach them how they contain themselves within themselves, and that the God-given force was going to rise up, but that they should be given the information that they are souls who have already experienced this force.

Too little attention, he believed, is given during the formative years to the biological conditions within the child. By the age of three, children know they are different from the animals. He said the animal instinct is the source of humankind's undoing. But the biological sexual urge is natural, and a child should be told early how to handle it when it awakens.

Children are capable of understanding responsibility, and they can be told from an early age that they are going to reproduce their own kind; that they will draw to them what they hold in their minds. Children can understand that fruits of the Spirit are just as much a part of their biological natures as is the sexual urge, and they can be taught to express gentleness, kindness, brotherly love, long-suffering, and so forth, as a method of setting into motion mental attributes that will build for them a kingdom.

Heredity, environment, and the people with whom we associate influence our faults, failures, and weaknesses. But the "way of escape" is prepared. "He hath not willed that any soul should perish," even through addictions.

Some incoming souls are attracted to an addictive family. Rather than lose spiritually by suffering addictions, the very purpose for being born might be fulfilled by the process of recovering from those very addictions seen as most destructive.

Heredity, environment, and the people with whom we associate also influence our character, integrity, and strengths. Spiritual development is not accomplished in placid peace, but in winning wars fought among various aspects of self.

How to Change Hereditary Influences

We can change hereditary influences by recognizing them as *gifts* and giving not only thanks, but *praise* for those we've been able to apply in soul development. As free-willed agents we don't *choose* what happens to us as children, but we do choose *how to feel* about what happened and about our hereditary influences. Our birth families are gifts we gave to ourselves before we were born.

Cayce said, "It is the spiritual activity within the body of the parents or the lack of it that determines the influence predominant in the life of their child." But as adults, nothing overcomes choice.

The Spiritual Family

Something wonderful is happening in our society.

Countless persons with a heritage of dysfunctions are discovering freedom from hereditary influences and claiming the inheritance that was meant for them—the right to choose. In our family relationships, it is important that we recognize the group as gathered for a purpose—in many cases, for the purpose of working out old hurts.

Where once we hid in closets, kept our secrets, and suffered in silence, never daring to admit we needed psychological and spiritual help, now we think nothing of hearing about famous people who've sought help for chemical addictions and so forth. We've literally come out of the closet and it seems a healthy trend, for it has enabled like minds to find each other, to become part of a familylike community of souls who are seeking to get on with it. It's the spiritual transformation, restoration, and recovery community, marked by small groups that don't cost money to join. The price of belonging is commitment to wellness.

We don't seem to need to share specific compulsions, only general backgrounds marked by repressed family attitudes, in order to recognize one another. Only for the past fifty years have we been capable of the instant communications that allow us to see inside one another's family lives. It also seems there has been an insurgence during this time period of souls who are highly aware and, frankly, fed up with the outrageous methods of not coping with life thrust upon us by traditional institutions, such as schools and churches. A groundswell of spiritually restored, mentally healthier individuals are making their presence felt among us. There are universal truths at work. The old order is falling to make way for the new.

Cayce spoke of this natural trend as leading to the comprehension and knowledge of the continuity of life and its experiences in the earth. We are gaining an understanding of our purpose for being here, and even though environmental and hereditary forces influence us psychologically, spiritually we sense that we have a choice about how we will allow these influences to affect us.

We are finally gaining enough insight and intelligence to recognize past dependency patterns, and are taking steps to remold the pattern into one that will carry us into the next century. Our educational system is recognizing that it has made few provisions for the child who hears his own music, and fewer for the child who thinks his own thoughts. Some of our churches are recognizing that if they are to remain a viable force for good, they must come to terms with the realities of today: that God is being perceived by many as personal, capable of communicating with His children directly, wherever they are, without intervention of clergy. Many are "seeing the light" literally.

The "light" is being shed on family systems that have, down through the ages, become distorted. No longer are we willing to pass on to our children bizarre rules that crippled us. We are reckoning with our denials, fears, compulsions, and avoidances of ourselves. We are making our own rules and re-forming our ideas about what a family should be: *a place where if it's important, it gets talked about, not ignored.*

Change appears to be slow in coming, but it isn't really, not when we consider how recently we've been able to be in touch with one another. One idea can present itself to more people in five minutes than it could in five hundred years before television.

We fly through the air to gather in groups to discuss subjects not even thought of fifty years ago. Then we come home and telephone our friends to discuss them further. We zing around like ricocheting cannonballs, picking up information, and we're *using* it, at least somewhat, to enrich our lives and the lives of those who will follow. And who will follow? Perhaps it is we who will follow.

As more and more people come to believe that we, as our own ancestors, created the world in which we live, we now believe that we can re-create it—that we don't have to destroy it as once seemed inevitable. We can preserve it for as long as it shall be preserved. It may not be given to us to know how long that is, but we will at least try to hand it back to God in as good a shape as it was handed to us.

We will fight for relationships with our families for the same reason we fight for our trees and wilderness and protect our animals as best we can.

We want them to be there when we return as our own heirs.

"The grave is not the goal."
1792-2

"Man is one name belonging to every
nation upon earth. In them all is one soul
though many tongues. Every country has its
own language, yet the subjects of which
the untutored soul speaks are the same
everywhere."
—Tertullian
[Quintus Septimius Florens
Tertullianus 160–240]

6

Secrets of the Soul's World

To the soul, there's no such thing as many lives, just one
life lived through many experiences.

The secret world of the soul is the fascinating realm of
the interbetween, the borderlands, the netherworld, where
phantasmic, shadowy, etheric, astral spirits wander among
the grateful dead.

Or, the secret world of the soul is the fascinating realm of
the interbetween, the borderlands, the netherworld, where
each of us finds what's been built by the soul's mind. The
story of the soul's world told in the Edgar Cayce readings is
your story and mine. It is a story you help to write.

The story of your soul begins when you were thought of
by the Creator. You began as a thought form in the Creator's

mind. Picture a blue sky filled with millions of floating bubbles, twinkling rainbow colors sparkling in the sunlight. You are one of those beautiful bubbles, fragile but happy and free.

But you couldn't stay in that form because you had something you needed to do. Eventually you found yourself inside a human body because that's where some of the work gets done. But not all the work is done there because, for one thing, human bodies can't fly, and you can.

Your body is composed of atomic energy particles visible to other souls, and sometimes to humans. Humans see you as filmy, whitish, translucent ectoplasm emanating from around the shoulders, if they are not afraid to look very closely, and if they hold very still so they don't disturb the vibration. They also may see you as a ghost. But the best thing about this body is that it's the temple of God whether you're in the earth or in the borderlands, in a physical body or out.

Another thing about getting the work done . . . human minds have so many distractions. Your real mind, the soul mind, concentrates better. Especially at night, when much of the earth clatter finally sleeps, you really can get busy, and you do.

In fact, any time you can get the bigmouths—the conscious and subconscious minds—to be *quiet* long enough to listen, you transmit instructions for carrying out your work. They don't obey orders well, but you do the best you can. These other two levels of mind come with the territory of earth. You like it better out in the borderlands, where it's just you and God, the two of you, talking things over, checking out your progress, making minor course corrections. You like it when the human body you're in learns to meditate because it gives you a chance to communicate. But you aren't stingy in your communiqués.

You begin to speak to your human compadre as soon as he or she develops a conscience. It's conscience that makes him or her curious about you. Your presence is sensed long before it's known who you are. Often you are discovered accidentally, such as in the instant between the moment it is known a catastrophe is about to happen and it happens. In that instant, the conscious and subconscious minds freeze, become paralyzed, and can't think. That's when you may jump in just in the knick of time to avert disaster. You like to help out that way. After all, if your human gets itself killed, you have to start over, and it's inconvenient. You have so much to do.

Under earth's noisy circumstances it's a wonder anything ever gets done. You remember when things were quieter. In fact, you remember every relevant thing since the beginning: all your trips through earth, whether you were a boy or a girl, or maybe you got mixed up a couple of times and didn't know which you were.

You remember what made you happy or sad, angry or fearful, whether what you did was useful in your real work, or was a real bust as incarnations go. You remember if you died in some significant way or merely faded into oblivion like a rose whose time is spent.

Your soul mind records descriptions of the environments it has experienced. Every place you've been since you were created is part of what you are today. Not quite like an old diary, these remembrances may be read by your conscious mind if it can tune in to where your soul mind stores the records—in between time and space. There is a "need to know" quality about these records. The soul mind doesn't tell the conscious mind everything; it all depends on the desires and purposes of your soul mind, and whether revealing the information would be helpful in getting on with the work.

Getting on with the work is the whole point of earth life. Learning to love is the work, and it's so difficult in earth, what better place to learn? Your task is to love as God loves—even those who call on other gods, and those who nurture satanic influences in direct opposition to the Christ Consciousness, which is your awareness of your eventual destiny.

Meanwhile, you zap around the cosmos, picking up influences here and there, associating yourself with vibrations that will fine-tune yours. You are always moving closer to the I AM or to involvement with your own ego, whether you're in earth or someplace else. You seek influences and experiences to prompt your own expression. If you are unbound by earthly ties you may express freely during sleep, meditation, or after the transition known as death. Instead of being lost in the maze of confusion and dissension that is often the human experience, you may know yourself as part of the whole, whether in or out of the body. While in the body your expression is limited to three or four dimensions. But out of body, in the borderlands, you can experience eight.

There are really nine dimensions, but we don't know much about the ninth, which seems to be final and disconnected from earth consciousness. But as a soul aware of yourself as you pass through material consciousness, you become aware of four levels of awareness operating in earth and four operating in "heaven."

These eight dimensions—earth is the third—exist so that every idiosyncrasy of every individual soul may be met from the beginning of time to the end as we know it. The Creator wishes that not a single one of us should perish, so these dimensions—also called systems—arouse the soul to its need to know its Maker.

All these systems exist in our own universe, of which science has yet to find the edge, and are represented by the planets and other heavenly bodies. Earth is special in being the only planet in our universe where we may live in human form. Life on the other planets consists of vibrations and influences. There are other universes beyond ours, but being concerned with them is like putting the cart before the horse. We will never see them if we don't choose whom we shall serve and complete the earth task of learning to love.

This business of eternal life is depressingly conditional. Either learn to love or else! About the most embarrassing thing that can happen to a soul is to get banished to Saturn. It's like having to stand in the corner till we say we're sorry. But that's not the worst thing that can happen. The absolute worst is to get blotted out. Vanquished. Gone. Burst like a bubble and that's that. Shudder at the thought.

Well, anyway, as I was saying, think of your trips through earth as a loop through the eight. Life is really all one, though only in earth do we take on a physical form and physical mind, to which we become inordinately attached, considering the scope of our existence. Our life is certainly not limited to earth influences.

Information is given in the Cayce readings concerning the following influences. The definitions that follow are from *The Random House Dictionary of the English Language, Second Edition, Unabridged:*

Arcturus—a first-magnitude star in the constellation of Boötes, known as the Herdsman, a northern constellation between Ursa Major and Serpens.

Planets—Jupiter, Mars, Mercury, Neptune, Pluto, Saturn, Uranus, Venus, and Earth.

Vulcan—a hypothetical planet nearest the sun whose existence was erroneously postulated by astronomers to account for perturbations in Mercury's orbit. In reading 826-8 Cayce said Pluto and Vulcan are one and the same.

Septimus—for which there is no dictionary definition, but is mentioned by Cayce in three readings as an influence.

Orion—a constellation known as the Hunter, lying on the celestial equator between Canis Major and Taurus, containing the bright stars Betelgeuse and Rigel.

Pleiades—a conspicuous cluster of stars in the constellation Taurus, commonly spoken of as seven, though only six are visible.

Polaris—the pole star or North Star, a star of the second magnitude situated close to the north pole of the heavens, in the constellation Ursa Minor: the outermost star in the handle of the Little Dipper.

Dog Star—the bright star Sirius, in Canis Major; also the bright star Procyon, in Canis Minor.

Included is information about the sun, the moon, and the twelve astrological sun signs and concepts, as well as cusps and constellations.

According to the readings, the soul has experiences and learns lessons from these planetary conditions, which it then brings into physical experience. These manifest as strong, unconscious influences on an individual's personality, character, urges, desires, habits, and preferences.

But nothing, the readings insist, equals or surpasses individual will, which directs what we do about what is known. Neither the date nor place of birth, the numerological conditions or positions of the planets actually direct the life being lived.

"The strongest power in the destiny of man is the Sun, first; then the closer planets, or those that are coming in ascendancy at the time of the birth of the individual; but let it be understood here, no action of any planet or any of the phases of the Sun, Moon, or any of the heavenly bodies surpasses the rule of man's individual willpower—the power given by the Creator in the beginning, when he became a living soul, with the power of choosing for himself."[1]

Each planetary influence—not the planet or star itself, but the influence—vibrates at a different rate. A soul entering that influence enters that vibration. It is the universal law of grace that the soul may at that time choose to become harmonious with the vibration or move on.

It's like reading a book:

We come under the influence of a good story much the same as though it were another place. Whether we decide to stay there and finish the book depends on whether the vibrations are harmonious with our own. We read by choice only because we are learning something, or because we want to experience life momentarily from the writer's viewpoint.

Planetary sojourns can be likened to book reading in that, as children, we are forced to read certain books considered necessary for our education. If we wisely realize that education is never-ending, we voluntarily read all our lives. At some point in our evolution we voluntarily place ourselves under the vibrations associated with certain planets, much in the same way we pick up a book. What we learn from either—and do about what we've learned—is our choice.

[1](254-2, Book 18, p. 493.)

Another way of putting it: Sojourns are short stays in environments being entertained by the body. This means the mental environment changes each time we admit into the mind these influences and conditions, and stay there for a time.

It works like this:

When we walk out of our homes into a theater and focus on a movie, the movie, so to speak, walks into us. Certain films have the ability to live on in us as memory, often altering our perception of life long after we've left the theater. We sojourn in the theater, and the film sojourns in us.

As books and films affect our thoughts, soul sojourns leave us with impressions and urges. In reveries, for example, the imagery can become so strong we have to "come back" from the beach or mountaintop, or wherever we have visited. Between earth lives these thoughts may be acted out and brought back in as inborn urges.

There exists in us from birth forces that impel us in one direction or another. Some of these drives are latent, such as artistic ability that is not pursued until late in life. Others manifest early, such as musical prowess. These urges may come from experiences between incarnations. We may feel the innate urges from other periods. To the soul there is no time, and no such thing as many lives. There is just one life, lived through many experiences. To evaluate these experiences, the soul calls on the sixth sense.

Sleep is when the sixth sense acts.

Cayce called sleep "a shadow of that state called death" because the physical consciousness becomes unaware of existent conditions, except for the parts of the physical mind that belong to the imaginative forces, which participate in dreams.

In the lowest to the highest animate beings, the five physical senses are on guard during normal sleep, especially the sense of hearing, which is most universal in aspect.

Generally, the other four senses of taste, touch, sight, and smell are less aware of what is taking place around the sleeping body. All the systems necessary to sustain life function; therefore, what sleeps is the sense of perception related to the physical brain.

During sleep the auditory sense becomes subdivided: we "hear" by feeling and smelling, and through all the senses that are independent of the brain centers themselves.

However, the sixth sense partakes of the auditory forces as dreams. The sixth sense also partakes of the accompanying entity that is ever on guard before the throne of the Creator itself.

The sixth sense is the very force of the soul in its experience, regardless of what that experience has been. It alters brain responses much like a string vibrates according to how it is tuned, but it functions in sleep as a sense.

It informs the soul much as the five physical senses inform the physical body. It communicates information to the soul as it goes out into that realm of experience which may encompass eons of time, and correlates the experiences of the soul according to its own accepted criterion or standard of judgments, in the same way your fingers inform you whether touch is pleasant or unpleasant. The sixth sense keeps the soul safe.

Just as physical senses can be sharpened—in effect, *trained* to see or hear, perhaps be more *aware* of certain sights or sounds—the sixth sense can be trained to monitor the soul's experiences.

Here's how:

We've all had the experience of falling asleep sorrowful and waking elated. What has happened? The sixth sense has evaluated the sorrow-causing experience, according to its own criterion, and reported its findings. Again, by analogy, your finger has touched something it thought was unpleasant and found it surprisingly pleasant.

Of course, it happens the other way around. We fall asleep peacefully and awaken depressed, lonely, hopeless, or fearful. What has taken place?

It could be an experience of which we are physically unaware, and that has not been remembered in a dream, but which must find its expression. Cayce said we set up warring conditions within the body if we set ourselves against the Creator's love. He said sleep is when the soul takes stock of what it has acted upon daily. The soul compares what it has done with what it knows to do. It abhors what has passed or enters into the joy of the Lord.

This is why the soul considers writing down dreams essential to self-preservation, as mentioned in "Secrets of Soul Guidance." We can learn more about the secret world of the soul through dream study than any other way.

Commonly considered merely intuition, the sixth sense is not intuition alone. If it were, it couldn't be trained.

A woman asked Cayce how to train her intuition. He answered, "Train intuition? How would you train electricity?"

He went on to make the point that intuition is not trained, but *governed* through ideals and purposes; by keeping the body, mind, and soul attuned to celestial forces rather than earthly forces; by listening to music that comes from the spheres.

In training the sixth sense, your desire governs. Constant mental visioning in the imaginative forces toward the desired experiences develops the ability of the sixth sense to assess the daily experiences of your soul. Your soul body is built by the impressions your soul mind receives.

The universal law of like begets like governs the character and content of dreams. In dreams, as well as in waking life, you father that perceived as needed to propagate yourself. If you sow the seed of honor you reap glory. Seeds of corruption produce a harvest of shame. Dreams are activities of your soul in the unseen world. It's a mistake to believe the dream world isn't real.

It is also a mistake to leave the sixth sense submerged, unnoticed, untrained. If left to its own initiative it makes war, expressed by disease, temper, and the whole host of negative emotions, especially anger and loneliness. This fact alone accounts for why it is essential to patrol your thoughts; to use the imaginative forces as aids to attunement to your ideals and purposes. These are what your soul cares about—the job it has to do. If the ideal is lost, the soul loses its ability to contact the spiritual forces.

A soul cut off from its Maker while in earth is miserable. We enter the earth in a body prepared by others. We leave the earth in the soul body we have prepared for the realm of the interbetween, wholly dependent on what we've done about what we know to do. In between there have been many choices.

These choices have two possible results:

"Go away, I never knew you."

Or, "Well done, good and faithful servant."

In the secret world of the soul, concern is for eternal life. The developed soul doesn't care about money, fame, and prestige. It cares about its true birthright: faith, freedom, and will.

The soul who has claimed its birthright knows that faith is like an unlimited bank account, where the more you spend, the more you have to spend. When you spend faith, it doesn't subtract from the balance, it multiplies. Unlike unspent money that grows by drawing interest, unspent faith shrinks. It doesn't vanish, however, because even orphan souls spend a tiny bit each day, even if unaware. Just by going to sleep each night humans show faith that the morning will come. If we didn't believe that, we wouldn't go to sleep.

The soul who has claimed its birthright knows that freedom comes from aligning with universal law.

The soul who has claimed its birthright knows that will is the gift of a loving Creator who dared risk losing us so that we might find ourselves. The consequences of misusing this heritage of will are no secret. We suffer them daily, every time we act on an impulse that contradicts the influences we would rather have shape our lives. In the secret world of the soul, misapplication of will actually separates us not only from our best efforts, but from the Infinite.

The hope of the soul is to become one with the spiritual mind that created it. Through telescopes scientists observe the spiritual mind at work creating new stars. We see it working in us when we, for instance, know things we haven't learned. The spiritual mind is perhaps most visible in earth's plant kingdom. Plants reproduce themselves by the same principles that govern the spiritual mind's creation of itself, the universal laws of attraction and like begets like.

Like the orchid that replicates a female wasp to assure its own pollination, we replicate ourselves so that what we need will be drawn to us. The orchid fathers itself by attracting the male wasp.

The spiritual mind of the universe is not the entire mind of the Creator. It was created by the Creator, the first creation, and is creative. Some other names for the spiritual mind are superconscious, mind of God or the Father, universal mind, Christ mind, the divide, the lamb, the Shepherd, the door, the way, the I AM, and Our mind, the Son.

The spiritual mind is the collection of all knowledge since the beginning. It is the barrier the soul's mind must cross to reach oneness. It is known as the door upon which the soul's mind must knock. Depending on the soul's purposes, the spiritual mind may function as a subconscious mind while the soul is in the borderlands. It answers the call of the soul's mind. It does not force itself on the soul. It waits on the other side of the door until called by some aspect of the soul mind.

The soul mind chooses to become one with the spiritual mind. The soul mind participates and collaborates in its own redemption from separation. The soul mind has the option to open the door to the spiritual mind, not the other way around. The final choice to open the door is made by the soul mind, often after collaboration with the conscious and subconscious minds. Opening the door is risky to the earthly subconscious mind because it doesn't want to give up what it thinks is control. But majority rules. If the soul mind and the conscious mind agree to open the door to the spiritual mind, the subconscious can't prevent it.

In the secret world of the soul, the soul can see that it is not perfect. Its thoughts are not always worthy of communing with the spiritual mind. It desires to nestle in the secret dwelling place for correction as well as comfort. In or on the soul mind is imprinted the pattern of the Christ, which it wants to manifest in light as well as in darkness.

The soul in its secret place understands Spirit (explored further in Chapter 18). Spirit is the soul's own soul. Other names for this Spirit are the universal soul, the soul-of-the-soul, the Oversoul, God's soul, Life's soul, Infinite energy, the Servant, the collective soul, the First Cause.

This Spirit is the Creator's own soul. The Creator's soul, the soul of the soul, and the soul of a tree are the same soul. It activates and animates all life nonselectively, impels infinity, develops the soul's mind when asked, and helps the soul to cross the divide to the spiritual mind, to the Son, the first creation.

The soul also understands that Spirit transformed through Christ is what makes Spirit holy. In fact, the Holy Spirit is the Christ's own soul. The soul understands that in the trinity of Father, Son, and Holy Spirit, Son is the mind of Father and Holy Spirit is the soul of Son. And that in the secret world of the souls *all* know of this truth, whether they act on it or not.

Acting on it is difficult in earth with all its distractions. But in lucid moments of awareness the soul makes its longings felt to express the secrets of its heart. If we hold very still, and listen very carefully, we can hear the soul saying, "Abba, Father. I surrender."

How to Free the Soul from Irrelevance

We can aid the surrender of the soul by consciously detaching from irrelevancy.

There you are, a soul in the borderlands, ectoplasmic energy, able to zap around probably rather effortlessly. Now, what are you thinking of? What are you thinking with? Are you thinking at all, or are you asleep?

Are you wishing you were back on earth? Remembering that so-and-so who messed up your life? Craving a chemical? Are you angry, confused, or whatever? If so, you are trapped in irrelevancy.

However, if you are detached from earth, but busily going about the soul's business, in total harmony with the cosmic consciousness, you may skip this section.

The soul mind remembers only what is relevant, but sometimes the snares of earth become relevant. As a soul, do you want to be encumbered by all that you have carried throughout your life in your subconscious mind? If not, you must detach from it now. For only through incarnations in earth can earthly things be met. It is imperative to recognize *now* what is real and to detach from all else as best you can.

A person who won't recognize what is real is like a woman whose house is on fire, but won't leave without her false eyelashes.

A person who won't detach from mental baggage is like a man walking through an airport dragging his house behind him.

A person who won't detach from irrelevancy is like the woman who had her dead husband stuffed and placed in a chair so she could yell at him some more.

The Bible simply says, "Leave the things of the earth behind." Cayce reading 281-39 says: "For thoughts are things, and the mind is the builder. But if ye fill thy mind with cares of the world day by day, ye may not in the moment give the best that is in the life of those that live the Christ life—even as Jesus gave the new commandment, 'that ye love one another.' "

The key phrase in this reading is "ye may not in the moment give the best." All we have is the moment to give. The moment. To give. Herein lies relevancy.

That's what it comes down to. The moment. This is how the past is built: moment by moment. This is how it is done. What *is* is the mirror that reflects *what has been* and *what shall be*. See it. Be it.

Make lists.

List circumstances, attitudes, emotions, traits, and habits that you wish to detach from. List also that which is pleasing to you and question if this is what you wish to carry with you from now on, remembering that to the soul there is no such thing as time and no more lives. This is it. The beginning and the end is *now*.

This listing is like pretending you are going to change residences (consciousness). You walk through the rooms of your house, deciding which furnishings you shall keep, which you shall leave behind. Liken your belief system, attitudes, and emotions to furnishings of your home. Is your home furnished with treasured antiques that have stood the test of time? Or old junk you never wanted but inherited from Aunt Mildred? Or snappy new plastics that are going to last about five minutes before they are dull and worn looking?

Now pretend that money is no object, and you are going to purchase new furnishings for your new residence (consciousness). The whole world is one giant department store and you can afford any or all of it. Would you go wild and take one of everything and worry later about where to put it? Or would you select time-honored craftsmanship in the style and color of your choice?

Would you give some thought as to how you want to live? You can afford it now, so what will it be? Your spiritual heredity of faith bankrolls the project. So go ahead and choose.

After this fabulous shopping spree, you are back at home in your old residence preparing for the move. You look around and there, among all your old stuff, is your favorite chair. Gosh, you can't leave that! Nothing new would be as comfortable. Fine. Take it with you. But first question whether you really, really love it, or are afraid of being out of your comfort zone. Will you cling to the old chair—regardless how shabby—out of love or out of fear? It is, after all, your chair, to do with as you choose. But remember, you are moving (in consciousness). That idea may frighten you so much that you, by golly, will take that chair. Just in case. You want something to remind you of the past no matter how shabby. That chair holds memories.

Old attitudes and beliefs are like that old chair. We curl

up in them and feel comfortable. Safe. We think nothing else could feel as safe as that old chair. Okay, it won't look right in the new place, but *I'm taking it with me anyway. I'll store it in the attic and bring it down if I feel like it.*

You can always slipcover it.

What was that?

Sure, you can put a fresh new cover on it so it won't look so shabby. Of course, underneath it's still the same old chair, only with a new face on it. That way you can hang onto it but no one will know. You can fool everybody. But you can't fool yourself. You'll know. But that's okay, too, if it is okay with you. You may vow to take that chair with you into eternity . . . and that's exactly what you will do. The attitudes we cling to and refuse to part with go with us. Just realize that if you decide to carry that chair, that attitude, with you into the borderlands, *it will be carried back with you into earth*. It will become a part of your mental heredity. It's a universal law.

What we hold in the mind becomes a part of the consciousness forever unless we discover a need to be rid of it. Then we must come back into the earth to discard it.

However, that old chair does not necessarily represent an attitude we need to be rid of. It could just as well be made of the right stuff to stand the test of time—the one thing that will get us through. "As a man thinketh in his heart so is he." That old chair could represent patient persistence, the attitude that in and of itself, if set in this direction, can enable us to first sort things out and, finally, to discard that which is undesirable.

So carefully list all the furnishings of your house (thoughts, feelings, attitudes, emotions, beliefs of your family consciousness). See them honestly. See which of them you want with you in the new place, be that new place a new awareness here in earth, or in the environs of the soul here in earth, or on sojourns elsewhere. As the soul sojourns elsewhere through dreams and meditation, while remaining attached to flesh and blood, detaching from cares of the world frees the soul to develop more fully.

A soul entangled in irrelevancy is bound and suffers. The

soul makes its suffering felt. The soul mind transmits its needs to the physical mind, but it has to make itself heard over the clatter in the subconscious mind. We can hear the soul crying in our loneliness.

When we break free of the cares that bind us to the earth, we can hear the soul's laughter in our joy.

7

Secrets of the
Little Choo Choo

He got right up that hill. Many of us are huffing and puffing, "I think I can, I think I can," believing, like the Little Choo Choo, that if we think we can, we can. We are told that if we put our minds to it, anything is possible. We are told to have faith in ourselves and believe in our abilities. It is called self-esteem.

Several fallacies about self-esteem are loose in the world. It even is getting dangerous.

One little girl I read about, whose mama told her she could do anything if she just set her mind to it, decided she wanted to fly. She jumped off the barn and broke her leg. This little girl decided her mama must have left something out, for she surely had set her mind to flying. She wisely decided there must be more to it.

But what is it?

It's universal law.

Cayce said, "Thoughts are things." The Bible says, "As a man thinketh in his heart so is he." The Bible also says, "Ye cannot change one whit by thought." Maybe we need to rethink both positions. There must be something in between "you can if you think you can" and "wishin' don't make it so." Maybe universal laws govern us and our thoughts; and if we could understand them, we'd find the middle road. If that road leads to accepting limitations, a very unpopular idea these days, maybe we would all be better off for it.

Giving up our dreams can't be right, but neither can jumping off barns. Maybe a piece of the answer lies in this verse:

> Thoughts are things
> not wings.
> We may think that we can fly
> but break our bones when we try.
> And no amount of do or die
> can stop our tears when we cry.
> Some thoughts push us to the brink
> where we can jump, or we can think.
> For some, thoughts are helpful all.
> For others, wild delusions stall
> as shackles bind and stifle life
> that could be lived in milder strife
> if only thoughts weren't things
> but *wings!*

And therein lies the problem. Thoughts aren't wings, but things. And things are limited in and of themselves. True, the mind is nearer limitless than anything in the universe, but even the mind is subject to universal law.

If the Little Choo Choo had decided he wanted to be a

Greyhound bus, he'd have been in big trouble. The reason he got up that hill is because he stayed on track.

"IF YOU CAN CONCEIVE IT, YOU CAN ACHIEVE IT!!!" is not universal law. It's media hype.

The idea is extremely seductive, but false. It's earth's fault. Only a distorted illusion of what the secret self, the true "I," can conceive can be manifested into earth. Our mental hospitals are filled with folks who disagree. Believe strongly enough that you're a bird and our society will put you in a cage. It sometimes has to do with being able to know the difference between earth sojourns and mental and spiritual sojourns in other environs, explored in the previous chapter. But the universal laws govern every phase of existence—physical, mental, and spiritual. Otherwise, chaos would truly reign.

Some thoughts are messages from the secret self. Some thoughts, being things, are like bolts out of the blue— profoundly insightful, meriting congratulations with much brouhaha all around. Other thoughts are like seeds broadcast through bird droppings. It is evidence of a loving Higher Intelligence that all seeds that drop from passing birds don't take root, as do not all thoughts. It would be rather horrible, I suspect, in our present state of development, if we could actually manifest solely by thought, with no concern for the outcome except our own interests. It would be nice if we could visualize someone's insides and rearrange their chromosomes, healing them as the Master did. But is that all we would do? Some days it's truly grace that I can't command water to turn into wine.

When we first get an idea, a thought, often we don't know for sure if it's a message from the secret self, a bolt from the blue, or seeds from a bird. Thoughts and ideas must be measured against our understanding of universal law.

Ask where the thoughts and ideas are coming from. If they are coming from within, fine. But look out for passing birds. True self-esteem comes when we stop feeling like failures because we did not do something that was never possible in the first place. In this life I am not going to be a size six, blue-eyed ballet dancer no matter how badly I want it. And *this* life is the one that *counts*.

Media would drown us in bird droppings if we let it.

Study universal law. There we are truly free. It's our spiritual heritage.

8
Secrets of Karma

First, what is karma?

A man asked Cayce how he could overcome karma. Cayce told the man he understood little the *meaning of karma*—it is that which is built by indifference to that known to be right. It is taking chances, promising to do better tomorrow.

"What is karma but giving way to impulse?"

A woman who asked what karma she had to overcome to free herself mentally and spiritually was told, "Karma is rather the lack of living that known to do. As ye would be forgiven, so forgive in others. That is the manner to meet karma."

"What is karmic debt? This ye have made a bugaboo!"

Another woman, this one with many problems, asked Cayce to tell her what her karma was so she could "strive" to overcome it. Cayce said instead of karma, she needed to overcome the fear and dread within herself. He said when we are living right, to disregard the fear of consequences is well. But when we disregard the consequences of "I," meaning *living for self instead of others,* we hit a "stone wall."

Cayce told another who asked whether she had "much bad karma to work out in this life," that "karma is rarely understood." He said, "Karma depends upon what the soul has done about that it has become aware of." He said karma isn't "worked out," it is forgiven.

"Forgiven" how?

Christ came into the earth, made Himself the law, and made it possible for us to approach the Throne of mercy, grace, and pardon, and know that all that we have been and done is washed away.

"He will stand in the stead. For, by sin came death; by the shedding of blood came freedom from a consciousness (of karma), into a greater consciousness (of grace)."

So it isn't that karma doesn't exist; it is rather that focusing on karma instead of Christ enslaves us. By seeking the Christ within we can then know that whatever must be met—and all must be met—is not bad karma but grace. The law of "reaping as we sow" is how we learn. The law of "like begets like" teaches us that we—not some karmic force—father our own creations. We have the choice of accepting responsibility for our actions and reactions, blaming someone or something else, or blaming God.

"Karmic influences must ever be met, but He has prepared a way that He takes them upon Himself, and as ye trust in Him He shows thee the way to meet the hindrances or conditions that would disturb thee in any phase of thine experience." This is grace.

Even focusing on or trying to create "good karma" still keeps the focus on self. Cayce told an eighteen-year-old female to "lose self in the consciousness of the indwelling of the Creative Force . . . in the channel prepared through the Son. Lose self; make His will one with thy will . . . and be a channel through which He may manifest. . . .''

"He is thy karma, if ye put thy trust wholly in Him. Not that every soul shall not give account for the deeds done in the body, and in the body meet them! But in each meeting, in each activity, let the pattern—not in self, not in mind alone, but in Him—be the guide.''

As long as we focus on self we may keep replaying the same old record, never allowing ourselves to hear music from other spheres. As soon as we look past the self, all the way inward to the Christ, new symphonies lift us out of the quagmire of the past. We no longer cast about alone seeking this or that. A relationship with the living Christ changes our responses to situations and circumstances. As the relationship matures and develops, and each situation and circumstance is seen as an opportunity to know Him better, karma is no longer relevant.

9

Secrets of Inner Fires
and Fears

Fear propelled me into the Edgar Cayce readings, and into attempting to discover the secrets of the universe. It was necessary to begin where I was, but I had to move ahead mentally from where I was before I could look back and identify where I had been.

Twice I have felt abject terror that I was about to be struck dead by God. The first time was around 1949. I was eight years old and our house was two blocks from a movie theater. During the night a storm blew up and lightning struck that theater. It exploded with a force heard for miles around, bouncing me out of bed. Certain the end of the world had come, I hit the floor on my knees, praying furiously to be forgiven for whatever sins I had committed that day. Only when I heard the fire truck sirens did I realize that a catastrophe had occurred, but it wasn't Armageddon. I was terrified of Armageddon. It would be years before I would look up the original Greek and discover that Armageddon wasn't a battle, but a sort of "gathering into a place"; and the seventh angel pouring out his vial into the air didn't mean doom but meant *to bestow or shed abroad unconsciously*. But I remember that fear.

The second time was fifteen years or so ago. A Buddhist friend and I had been discussing the Christ. I'd tried to keep an open mind as she'd explained her beliefs, and thought I was doing well, until later, in meditation, I decided to ask Spirit if she was correct. I prefaced the question with something like, "If Jesus isn't the Christ as Judy says . . ."

Suddenly, in the altered state of meditation, feeling completely open and vulnerable to Spirit, I was gripped by a force and pushed backward in the chair. What felt like liquid fire seemed to be surging in my veins as though I were being devoured by a raging heat. A voice that can only be described as masculine and angry thundered inside my head: "Don't you ever question if Jesus is the Christ. He *is*."

The voice then said, "I will forgive you this once for I understand that you are practicing being open-minded and tolerant. I salute your efforts to become more loving. The beliefs of others are no concern of yours. I will deal with them in my own good time. But for *you*, Jesus is The Christ. Doubt it again and I will obliterate you from the body." Spirit does have a way of putting things.

I don't know how long I sat in that chair, shaking and terrified. That was my one and only direct encounter with what I believed then was an angered Holy Ghost. Years later I came across a reading that said never to doubt whether Spirit answers:

"Doubt not! For he that looks back, or doubts, is worse than the infidel. Remember Lot's wife!"

I will never forget the feeling of fire in my veins. I have no difficulty imagining that Lot's wife felt that fire just before she turned into a pillar of salt.

I have not "looked back" since. Though I have never forgotten the fear, I no longer fear the fear. I have come to understand it, even treasure it.

When I first heard of Edgar Cayce, now some eighteen years ago, I approached the readings with judicious fear. I cast a skeptical, jaundiced eye at ideas such as that we are attracted by the vibrations of our parents, or that we are not victims but rather participate in our own environment for the purpose of learning lessons. But the idea of reincarnation kept drawing me in. Even though I was expecting to be vanquished for blasphemy, I couldn't stop studying. Finding out the truth seemed worth the risk. I seem to have come in with two traits: I think I was born seeking Christ but also remembered living before, though not during the time of Jesus' ministry. In unquenchable curiosity, I pressed on, spending two years reading Jess Stearn, Thomas Sugrue, Gina Cerminara, and Hugh Lynn Cayce. *Edgar Cayce on Atlantis* was my favorite. But just to be on the safe side, I kept a Bible and a Billy Graham Bible Study Handbook nearby, to reference scriptures, and to try to catch Cayce in an outright lie. If you can't trust Billy Graham . . . ? I wanted to put such "foolishness" out of my mind and, as my Dad is so fond of saying, "get back to basics."

Traditional, fundamentally religious "basics," however, such as the good go to heaven and the bad go to hell, couldn't account for when this was supposed to happen, as I seemed to remember being someplace else in between lives on earth. Some impressions and memories seemed too vivid to be attributed to an overactive imagination. Cayce's version of creation was the most bizarre theory I'd ever heard, but to my eventual relief, not one word of it could be proved or disproved either by the Bible, or by my trusty Billy Graham Handbook.

When Cayce said the sixth-day creation was that of the souls, and that we were all "thought up" by God at the same time, I could picture souls floating like bubbles blown out of the mouth of God in the first chapter of Genesis. When Cayce said that we souls began creating on our own, entering the bodies of animals and becoming trapped in them I recalled mythological creatures that fill historical literature. When Cayce said that God had to make Adam and Eve to show us how we were supposed to look and function, suddenly the second chapter of Genesis made sense:

In the fifth verse of the second chapter of Genesis, "there was not a man to till the ground." Theologians have produced volumes trying to explain the discrepancy between this verse and Genesis 1:27, where "God created man in his own image. . . ." It became apparent that if such learned persons were unable to agree on when and how we began, it clearly was beyond my comprehension, and probably didn't matter anyway. Though an inner fire still compels the quest, the point seems moot when compared with why we are here and where we are going. How and when pales in the light of why. The *why we are here* and *what is ahead* compel us to ponder instead how to fulfill the potential and purpose for which we were created—which is, according to Cayce, to be companions to the Creator. This is a God to be feared?

Fear of God and the world is a symptom of thinking solely with the physical mind.

Recent developments in child psychology seem to indicate that we are born not as blank slates, as was once thought, but with distinct preferences and personalities. If we can learn, perhaps through dreams, about our mental and spiritual heritage—what we created and brought with us— we can, as adults, use the information as a means to discover our true natures. If part of our baggage is fear, we can begin to sort through it and discard those fears no longer perceived as needed.

Wherever we stand, even in fear, is Holy Ground. When fear is disdained as totally negative and unnecessary, a vital human element is invalidated. Fear is basic to survival in all animals. But we are souls living inside animal bodies. It's when we project Christ, through the use of will and mind, that the lower nature is subdued and fears subside. We can become grateful to our former fears when they at last are far enough behind us that we are able to turn around and see them for what they were: teachers. When the student is ready, the teacher appears, and disappears.

Children can be teachers, and "Thoughts are children of the mind and soul."

Fear of God and the world is one of the childish things we put away as soul develops. If allowed to remain too long, fear itself becomes our motivation and the greatest obstacle to fulfilling the purpose for life. I know. I became dependent on fear as though it were a friend. It isn't. Fear of the world is the enemy. It's the greatest destructive force of man's intelligence. Fear is co-dependent on us. Unless we permit, fear can't exist in us, can't feed off us.

Hugh Lynn Cayce, from the podium, looked me square in the eye one night during a lecture, and said, "Never feed a thought form. It will take you *over!*"

I never did know how he knew.

Fear itself can be viewed as a monstrous thought form, a vampire draining the life from us for its own sake. We build it, create it, and nourish it until it grows so large it becomes the spirit which directs how our lives will go. Once we give it life, fear entangles itself into our flesh and distorts our vision. It grows a voice louder than our own until we begin to think it is our own. The voice of the spirit of fear speaks through our mouths in subtle little ways that we don't even hear:

We say, "I'm afraid of what will happen if I do this or that." And, "Gee, I'm afraid I really don't know." Or, "I'm afraid you'll have to ask Mr. So-and-So."

We've accepted the language of fear as though it were meaningless.

EDGAR CAYCE FOUNDATION and
A.R.E. LIBRARY/CONFERENCE CENTER
Virginia Beach, Va.

OVER 50 YEARS OF SERVICE

BUSINESS REPLY CARD
First Class Permit No. 2456, Virginia Beach, Va.

POSTAGE WILL BE PAID BY

A.R.E.®
P.O. Box 595
Virginia Beach, VA 23451

785-71

We use words such as "God" in the same way we use words such as "afraid": "God, if I only could finish this project . . ." or "Good Lord, why in the world would you ask that?" As appeals to the Deity become meaningless, our lives become increasingly empty, and we seek other mirrors out there to reflect our existence.

The growing propensity for horror movies and books suggests that we are fascinated with fear. Could that be because it's an emotion with which we are so familiar that we feel comfortable in its presence? Have we trembled in its presence for so long we no longer notice the tremor? Have we not created a nation where fear stalks the streets in the bodies of souls who have given themselves over completely to fear? Do we not accept door locks as an acceptable part of life? We barricade ourselves behind fortresses designed to keep out robbers, murderers, and rapists whom we know lurk nearby because we read about our neighbors' misfortunes daily. We hope and pray it won't happen to us, but we fear it. However, fear of persons with a mental aberration always creates activity in the mind of those feared. Cayce said the way to protect ourselves, to offset and avoid such influences, is to "keep the eye single . . . in service for spiritual understanding."

We fear not only others but ourselves because we were created by a God we don't understand. We've witnessed the powers of nature and believed that these are the forces of a raging, vengeful God. We've seen disease ravage the bodies of loved ones and have railed against a learned version of God who could heal them if He would, so *why doesn't He?* How could a God be loving who could let a little child suffer? We fear ourselves because we've been taught that God is awesome and terrible, and we as His children are equally capable of meanness. We fear our own potential for destruction.

How can we love such a God; therefore, how can we love ourselves?

Such as we must be harnessed, shackled, and bound, lest we inflict some terrible pain on another. How could a God who would let his own Son die be worthy of loyalty? And so we feel alone. Abandoned. Separated.

This fearfulness can be replaced by an awe-filled respect for the majesty of our Creator as latent, previously subjugated creative energies begin to awaken and emerge into physical awareness. Gradually we may become less dependent on childhood experiences, teachings, and influences.

And less dependent on the conscious mind. Robert Frost said, "Nature is always hinting at us."

The physical level of mind, consciousness while awake, is in some ways more of a mystery than the mental and spiritual levels. The physical mind seems to sit on a stem like a flower head, showing its face to the morning, but closing its many petals at night. Like a flower, the physical mind develops through—and is so easily influenced by—environment. Some flowers—and minds—do best in a greenhouse; some thrive wild and free in a field. And like a flower, the color and texture of the physical mind depends on being fed both from above and below. The physical mind exists between earth and sky. Cut off from its source of nutrients before its time, it withers and dies.

The bedeviling truth is, of course, that like a flower, the physical mind is doomed to die anyway, eventually, regardless of the tender loving care it receives. That's what makes it different from the soul mind, which doesn't die unless it chooses to. Cayce said, "Selfishness is the basic sin and the soul that sins shall die."

Helmholtz called this inevitability of death "The Principle of the Conservation of Force":

"Nature as a whole possesses a store of force which cannot in any way be either increased or diminished . . . therefore, the quantity of force in Nature is just as eternal and unalterable as the quantity of matter. I have named this (a) general law."

More recently, Loretta's mother in the film *Moonstruck* put it succinctly when she told her husband, who was cheating on her, trying to stay young because he was afraid of death, "Cosmos, you're gonna die no matter what you do."

It has been our human nature to fear death, but a worse fear, more difficult to overcome, is to fear life. Lewis Thomas says this is because "we are, perhaps uniquely among the earth's creatures, the worrying animal. We worry away our lives, fearing the future, discontent with the present, unable to take in the idea of dying, unable to sit still."

It is difficult to comprehend without some element of fear creeping in that the physical mind and body is where death takes place, even though death begins the day we are born. We'd rather not believe the clock ticks on in a race against death which cannot be won. Why don't we know that and act like it? Why do we think of ourselves as gods?

"Don't act like ye think ye are a god! Ye may become such, but when ye do ye think not of thyself."

Why don't we realize the earth is the valley of the shadow? We're Shakespeare's "cowards (who) die many times before their deaths," who never fully learn to live. This is the fiercest trap even for those who believe in reincarnation.

To postpone life until next time—when there is no guarantee of next time—is death by burial alive. We can choose not to live, but we can't choose not to die physically.

The error is in believing we don't have to live because we are not going to die.

Like Cosmos, we're "gonna die no matter what we do." Not living physically is to die spiritually. We act as though the two were mutually exclusive, when really, spiritual eternity depends on the physical reality now.

The reality is, while we have little to say about physical death, we have everything to say about the continuity of life on the other side. There's our bailiwick. There is where the good times never end.

Cayce repeatedly mentioned Deuteronomy 30, verses 15 through 20, which translate into "today is set before thee life and good and death and evil; therefore, choose life and good."

Today is the operative word here because what is going on in the physical mind today is building the remaining tomorrows, both here and on the other side. That's why today desperately matters. There is no promise of tomorrow, in the Bible, the Cayce readings, or any of the ancient writings, without and unless certain actions are taken *today*. Knowing that but doing nothing is the cause of fear.

Sufficient unto the Moment Is the Evil...

One day at a time, huh? When it comes to conquering fear, how about breaking it down into ten-minute segments?

One of the best-known philosophies of living in the now is the twelve-step programs' "one day at a time" approach to life, based on the universal law of truth. There are truths to earn every single day.

Truth is earned, not learned.

Recognizing that today determines tomorrow, spiritually developing, recovering humans learn to think physically transcendent thoughts and take steps toward "putting away childish things (meaning things that happen as a child, such as crippling abuses)," and learn to attune to the Infinite.

Fears are replaced by gently burning fires of freedom after we accept the truth about ourselves.[1]

Others, waiting for a metaphysical experience—some beautiful, mystical revelation that can be perceived through

---

[1](John 8:32: "And ye shall know the truth, and the truth shall make you free.")

the physical mind before acting to overcome fear—are, in reality, looking for a shortcut. It's a universal law that there are none. But the path to freedom from fear is well worn. And there's lots of help along the way. As I said, I know. I've been there.

10

Secrets of Serenity

The secret to serenity is doing what you know to do about what you know so that you can be what you want to be. It's letting others be.

In 1928 Cayce told a man who'd lost the desire to live to take stock of himself, to take an inventory of his abilities and desires, then let go of the need to have confidence in others in order to live his life. He said to look at the world however he found it most interesting, then assume responsibilities and live up to them. Cayce said if he'd serve others, he'd form a relationship with himself; that the confidence and trust he'd lost in others must stop being a criterion for his own peace of mind.

Our problem today is we often don't comprehend "service to others." We're so ticked off at what others have done to us, the last thing we want to hear about is serving them or anybody else. But Cayce said service to others includes *putting the responsibility for the harm on the one doing the harm*.

That doesn't mean *blame* in the accusatory sense. It does mean *stop enabling people to hurt us by rescuing them from themselves*. It means letting go of the belief that we must "help" others because they won't survive if we don't. It means recognizing our participation in our own pain. It means to stop participating in theirs.

The Cayce readings contain the serenity principles that have been presented so lovingly throughout the world in Twelve Step meetings for more than half a century. Universal Truth is Universal Truth, regardless from whence it comes.

It comes from within. All the serenity, all the truth, all the peace, all the questions and all the answers are inside, sitting right alongside the pain and all its attendant emotions. But we can't see the peace unless we're willing to look at the pain. They are so closely related it's hard to tell which is which.

To have inner peace and serenity does not mean to sleepwalk through life like a zombie, glazed-eyed and numb, unaware of reality. It certainly doesn't mean ignoring the plight of others, explaining away poverty and pain as karmic justice. It doesn't mean walking away from trouble, nor does it mean "fixing" trouble—our own or someone else's. It does mean doing what we know to do *about what we know* so that we can be what we want to be—and letting others be.

Inner peace is about power—and letting go of the lie that we or anybody else has any. God has the power. All of it. But that doesn't make us powerless. To the contrary. Tapping into that makes us magnificently powerful—and at times, rather glorious. There is a particular glory that surrounds the person who surrenders in humility his or her past and future mistakes and embraces the beautiful pain of the moment. Beautiful because we cry in pain and we cry in joy and the crying is the beginning of trying—not to make it go away, but to walk courageously through it, feeling every nuance, every speck of what there is to feel. The willingness to walk through the pain is the secret to healing life's hurts. We can't feel the peace until we've felt the pain and let go of what's causing it. The pain comes out first and peace follows.

The cause of pain is some aspect of self. But we can't let go of self until we have a self to let go of. That means own, claim, and embrace every element that makes up life. Write about it in journals; talk about it in small groups of like-minded souls. Get a handle on where the pain is coming from and learn how to let the pain go.

Our pain comes from not letting go until we've reached the end of the rope. There we hang, suspended in space, hoping time will stop until we find the courage to turn loose. But time won't stop. It marches on and we get left behind.

Doing what you know to do about what you know becomes easier when you stop trying to do what's traditionally expected. Your values may agree with traditional expectations or they may not. For most of us, what we *know* changes alarmingly often. That's when living the principles works best. We are not required to have all the answers. God does not expect of us what we do not expect of ourselves, but what we expect of ourselves, God expects of us. So it's essential to clarify what that is.

How to clarify your expectations of yourself, do what you know to do, and be what you want to be, has already been outlined in ''Secrets of Soul Guidance,'' the second chapter. In fact, every chapter contains principles to help you think through this business of inner peace. It's serious business. Destiny depends on it. Wars in the outer world are but shadows of wars in the inner world. Your personal peace contributes in a very real way to world peace. Cayce suggests that personal peace in sufficient numbers of us is the secret to peace on the planet.

Personal peace comes from taking the focus off yourself and putting it onto others. Yet personal peace comes from taking the focus off of others and putting it on yourself. That's the dichotomy of humanness. If you can't help yourself, you can't help someone else; but if you can't help someone else, you can't help yourself. We are all in this thing together.

Knowing the best way to help is the trick. In fact, *knowing* is trickiest of all. Cayce's consistent message is: It is better not to know than to know and not do. For instance, one of the things we in our society generally know is that lying is wrong. That means telling the truth must be right. Then, it is better not to know the truth than to know it and not tell it. Whew! Talk about responsibility! Who wants to call *that* shot when telling the truth could result in our lives being blown to hell?

Now, don't misunderstand. It isn't likely that we know anything resembling truth about anyone but ourselves. If we think we know the truth about someone else, we're making judgments we probably aren't qualified to make. But we surely do know the truth about ourselves—at least partly. The best of us are keeping secrets, lying like rugs to that mirror every morning. We shine up our faces, put on those masks, and greet the day with hearts full of guile and guilt, then wonder why serenity eludes us.

The universal law of truth works two ways: It sets us free, but freedom is the last thing some of us want. Freedom involves too much personal responsibility. So we give power to the lies the same way we give it to people. We say, "I give you power over me because then you have to take care of me. That means I don't have to accept responsibility for my actions. If I misbehave, it's your fault!"

Empowering lies are peculiarly common. In some strange, odd way, we believe they protect us. But the last four letters of "peculiar" spell liar. Serenity requires that we stop lying to ourselves. We aren't required to confess publicly, only privately, to ourselves. (Don't worry. God already knows.)

Only after we truly accept the truth about ourselves can we stop blaming everybody else for our lack of serenity.

Then magic happens. The mass of tangled emotions begins to unravel one thread at a time. We have the privilege of following those threads to their very end to see where they lead, then coming back to pick up another one if we like. Where truth leads is up to us.

If life as we know it gets blown to hell, maybe it needs to. Maybe that life is filled with structures that have outlived their usefulness. Remember, wrecking balls and dynamite clear the way for new building. Where is it written that what was must always be?

We cling to attitudes, emotions, habits, people, places, and things as though life depended on them, when really, life depends on letting go of the old. We stand with our hands *and minds* firmly clutched, gripping, closed, around that old rope, unable to receive anything new unless and until we turn loose.

When something in your life needs to change it is always, always, always *you*, never the other guy. Never. It's your responsibility to find the courage to stop being someone's dart board. Or maybe it's you throwing the darts. Whatever the situation, *courage* is the key word to serenity. And here is the key question: *What is the most loving thing I can do in this situation?*

The answer is likely to be preceded by, *Find the courage to. . . .*

> Find the courage to go.
> Find the courage to stay.
> Find the courage to say yes.
> Find the courage to say no.
> Find the courage to hold on.
> Find the courage to let go.
> Find the courage to act.
> Find the courage not to act.
> Find the courage to speak.
> Find the courage to shut up.

This last one is the hardest for most of us. Just shutting up about something is almost impossible. How can we just stand quietly by and let someone do something utterly stupid? Did you ever stop to think that your yakking about it constantly is driving them to it? That if you'd shut up, lighten up, give the guy or gal a break, and have a little more faith, things might work out? Did it ever occur to you that others might know what they're doing, but that their path is different from yours?

I speak with particular authority on this subject. Those amens you hear are coming from Beloved and three sons.

"Thoughts unexpressed may sometimes fall back dead, but God Himself can't kill them when they're said," wrote Will Carleton.

Omar Ibn Al-Halif said, "Four things come not back: the spoken word, the sped arrow, time past, the neglected opportunity."

I invite you to never neglect the opportunity to *shut up*. It helps.

Besides, the late Hugh Lynn Cayce used to say, "Don't worry about what other people do. They can't get themselves into more trouble than they deserve."

You have to trust the universal law of grace and mercy to give them another chance, expressed best in, "Do unto others as you would have them do unto you."

I don't know whom to credit for this line, but somebody once said, "I consider myself to be a monument to trial and error." *There* is a person who has serenity. Acceptance of success and failure—our own and others'—letting everybody do and be as they see fit, is part of peace. Another part of peace is the universal law of consistency.

The Law of Consistency in the Search for Peace

Because I have a searching mind but a simple one, this book almost didn't get written. As I was working with the word *consistency*, which in addition to meaning "a steadfast adherence to a principle," also means "agreement," it became clear how the universe conspires to teach us its secrets.

It had occurred to me that the entire planet revolves around agreement: Buy/sell agreements govern finance; peace agreements govern foreign policy; babies get born because of agreement between sperm and egg, and so on. The Universe said, "Let's bring it down to where she can understand it," and before I could turn around, a veritable fury of disagreement swept through my kitchen. I'll spare you the details. Suffice it to say Beloved and I got into a fight, the dog—around whom the household had long ago agreed to turn—disappeared, and a sheriff appeared at my door, but not to return my dog.

I had discovered the line in the Edgar Cayce readings were he advised someone to pursue the "law of consistency in the search for peace." Intrigued, I suspected that I wasn't, at least in the sense of steadfastly adhering to a principle, but I wouldn't have pled guilty to being generally disagreeable. Well, only occasionally.

The law of consistency is simply behavior agreed upon and deemed necessary by at least two of the three levels of self, and if acted out regularly, produces a feeling of well-being, serenity, and peace.

Agreement, or harmony among the parts of a complex thing, heralds peace: a nonwarring condition, a state of mutual harmony.

Outwardly, peace is freedom from civil commotion, disorder, insecurity, strife, and dissension.

Inwardly, peace is freedom from annoyance, distraction, anxiety, and obsession. It is characterized by tranquility, serenity, stillness, silence.

When we are at peace, we are in a state of nonbelligerence or concord; we are untroubled, tranquil, content, and secure. *And probably dead.* There is little lasting peace in the earth for most of us, for, as Cayce said, "when we are without crosses, we have ceased to be of notice, and are no longer among the sons."

But the "crosses" don't necessarily destroy serenity and they serve a purpose; as for what, that's between each person and God. Here is a way to bear them more peacefully.

The Cayce formula for peace:

1. Unconditional surrender to Divine Mind.

2. Stop *trying* to be and just *be*.

3. Study "portions—any portions" of the Bible, *believing*, without making deals with God, that what you need will be given.

4. Make sure your words and actions agree with your purposes.

This is not intended as some glib catch-all, solve-all-problems list. All four steps are simple, but extremely difficult to do day in and day out without fail. But the higher degree of consistency with which they are practiced, the more they work, especially number four. Even during serene times, we can shatter our own peace by violating this one. (That's what I did, but the sheriff forgave me and went away peacefully. Shortly thereafter, a neighbor returned the dog.)

Our serene moments are treasures, to be sure, portends and promises, foreshadows of the infinite, to be entertained often in our minds. But when disharmony returns, at whatever level, for whatever cause, we have placed it before us for our own learning. Like a stern taskmaster, the disruption of peace within us drives us hard, presses us onward to learn, to become. We are ever becoming. We exemplify the process of change.

Change comes hard. To make our nature different from what it is, or what it would be if left alone, requires a reason. How to do it is one thing; why to do it is something else. We know how to do many things we don't do because we can't think of a reason why.

In the end, God is the why.

We know how to obtain personal peace, but we seem to forget why we should practice patience, love, kindness, gentleness, long-suffering, and brotherly love, which in and of themselves are the law of consistency in the search for peace.

We can't buy or borrow peace. We may clothe ourselves in the outward appearance of peace and show a facade to the world, but inwardly we know the difference. Peace doesn't hang on a rack, it comes from within. We must make peace ourselves with the warring factions within, then with others.

The soul is clothed in "skin and flesh,"[1] but God can manifest through us when we are "clothed in humility."[2] We display humbleness to the world, when we, though we know ourselves to be divine, are not proud or arrogant because everyone else is divine, too.

The first definition of divine is simply "pertaining to a god, especially the Supreme Being." Who among us does not pertain somehow to the Supreme Being? Therefore, humbleness, humility, and agreement are logical.

Disagreement appears to be illogical. It makes no sense for races to war against one another. We incarnate into a particular race for the opportunities each presents.

In nature, when the earth disagrees with the rain, floods occur. Then the water seeks its own level through an agreement with gravity.

In world affairs, nations agree not to blow one another up.

In relationships, we agree or disagree on how to spend vacations, which channel to watch, which restaurant to go to, which movie to see.

In the psychic, agreement between soul and body creates miraculous peace in the mind.

The Secret Shift

A secret shift in consciousness is taking place.

The "catasclysmic prophecies" in the Edgar Cayce readings, as well as other legends and prophecies from around the world, agree there exists the possibility for a disaster. However, "possibility" does not mean *absolutely*, and the call has gone out for those who will to participate in the shift in consciousness necessary to prevent calamity.

This shift is probably most adequately described in this book in chapter 15, "Secrets of the Bible," in the section

---

[1](See Job 10:11.)
[2](See Peter 5:5.)

titled, "Journey into Consciousness." By following the flow of the rivers out of Genesis, we arrive in Revelation, where those who will may walk with purpose into the light.

But many are feeling and hearing the call this minute wherever they are. As Cayce said, "Sing Sing or Timbuktu . . . the Lord is the God of the Universe." It becomes a practical matter to answer this call, and heed the soul's cries for action to stem the tide of what some feel will be destruction.

To answer the call, we begin to act lovingly, first to ourselves, then to others, until unending love surges around the planet through prayer and helpful communications between like minds—here a little, there a little, line upon line, precept upon precept.

Make the phone calls, write the letters, lift up in light, *be* the light to someone.

Count no effort, no matter how seemingly small, as lost. I've seen one smile totally transform the consciousnesses of twenty people standing in a stalled line—at least for the moment. But even that is a start. To speak one friendly word to a stranger is to participate in the maintenance of peace on the planet. It's a way of doing what you know to do about what you know, so you can be what you want to be—serenely alive and free.

11

Secret of the Mountain

There is a mountain of difference between faith and belief, which lies between us and progress:

A man climbed a steep mountain, which was treacherous and fraught with death-defying dangers. He reached the pinnacle, only to realize there was no place left to go. If he tried to climb back down, he faced the same dangers he'd met on the way up. He didn't want to go back; he wanted to go forward. Yet stretched between himself and the next mountain was a vast span of nothingness, a chasm impossible to cross.

While pondering his dilemma, he realized another fellow was standing alongside him, holding a wheelbarrow. The fellow pulled out of his pocket a ball of wire. He attached a large weighted hook to the end of the wire and flung it across the chasm. The hook clunked into yon mountainside. The fellow then walked the wire to the other side, pushing the wheelbarrow ahead of him.

The man watched, astonished, as pretty soon the fellow came back, still pushing the wheelbarrow ahead of him. The fellow said to the man, "You can do that, you know."

"But I have no wire, no wheelbarrow, no hook," the man said, trembling with doubt.

"You can use mine," said the fellow.

"I wouldn't want to take yours," said the man, trying to sound brave, but feeling quite desperate.

Then the fellow asked, "What is it that you want to happen?"

The man thought about it and answered, "I want to get to the other side."

The fellow said, "I happen to be going that way. Get in. I'll carry you."

"Oh, no. No. I wouldn't want to put you to that trouble," the man said, feeling his heart would burst from the fear.

"You don't believe I can carry you across?" the fellow asked.

"Oh, sure, sure," said the man. "I just saw you cross the ravine without effort. I'm sure I wouldn't be too heavy for you. I believe you can do it."

"But you have no faith that I can do it with you in the wheelbarrow," said the fellow, looking into the man's heart.

"Here's the way it shakes down," said the fellow. "To get to the other side, you can either climb back down this mountain, gather the tools and the skills that I already have, and do it yourself, or you can put yourself into this wheelbarrow, into my hands, and let me carry you across. Now, what will it be? It's your decision."

The "fellow" in this story represents any number of names by which we know the Superior Being: the Higher Power, the God Within, or the Lord's Christ, Jesus, which was whom I was told the fellow is when I heard the story as a child. Regardless by which name the "fellow with the wheelbarrow" is known (and please don't get bogged down in the masculine gender), the point is the same: We *believe* in the existence of a helper, a rescuer, but we don't trust that help with our lives. We don't have faith in the principles, skills, and tools, even if we've witnessed the unbelievable. So we climb up and down the mountain—the same old mountain—hoping it will be different this time. What do we think? That the mountain is going to move?

The secret of the mountain is that it isn't going to move.

The mountain is the mountain, just as life is life. The mountain *is* life, and there's no way around it. It isn't going to change. We must change. We must get in the wheelbarrow and hang on if we are going to cross the chasm.

There is another point here, though: The fellow with the wheelbarrow told the man he could learn to do that. The man couldn't conceive of himself becoming a fellow with a wheelbarrow. The chasm looked impassable, even after he was shown that it was not. The good news is that the fellow gave the man a choice. He didn't say the *only* way the man was going to cross that chasm was to do it himself. He could opt for being carried across. Either way he could get where he wanted to be. The difference here is a matter of degree. Do we want to get there, or do we want to get there, then come back and help others get there? If we truly want the latter, then we have some skills and tool gathering to do. Either way we need faith that the hook will hold.

The secret is to put your faith in the hook, not the mountain. The mountain doesn't care. The hook does. The mountain is not God. The hook is God. The fellow with the wheelbarrow put his faith in the hook. Why would we do otherwise?

12

Secrets Grandma
Didn't Know

As a child I occasionally accompanied my grandmother to Sunday night healing services at the Pentecostal church. There, those on stretchers would be rolled in and positioned in front of the altar. The preacher would shout and hoot and holler, sometimes speaking in tongues, and every so often somebody would get up and fall out in the aisles.

It might be necessary to duck as crutches flew through the air, having been thrown by one who no longer needed them. Once I inquired as to the advisability of wearing football helmets to the meetings, but Grandma said it wouldn't be necessary, that God would protect us from flying crutches. Well, Grandma, you were right.

During the services, whenever someone who had come in

on a stretcher was healed and walked out, it was said to be a show of great faith. Whenever someone who had come in on a stretcher was not healed, he or she was rolled back out with more or less of a "better luck next time." I inquired why some were healed and some were not. Grandma said those who weren't healed probably just didn't have enough faith. Well, Grandma, you were wrong.

Cayce said some people have enough faith to stay sick.

Such as when Jesus let Himself die on the cross.

He could have saved Himself but didn't. He had the power, but didn't use it. He let go of it for the greater good of all. He couldn't demonstrate how to resurrect unless He died. But even He had his moments.

In John 12:27, He said: "Now my soul is troubled; and what shall I say? Father, save me from this hour? But for this cause I came unto this hour."

What was He supposed to do? Back out and blow His chance? Hardly. He had the power and knew it. It would hardly have helped if He'd used it to save only Himself.

Children, most of all, demonstrate the same power. When a soul enters a newly created vessel that is deformed, or whose brain is hopelessly scrambled, who is to say that soul has not taken that on to demonstrate something to the caregivers? Who is to say that inside that pitiful-looking human is not a soul with the power to save itself, but does not? Does not that soul mirror something within ourselves? Provide us with an opportunity to search within? Give us this day the very bread that we need to inspire research? Compassion? Gratitude? Yes, gratitude for our own blessings.

And who is to say that a person who develops an illness such as cancer is not a soul testing its mettle? How do we know faith unless we tackle a biggie? How do we know what we're made of unless we really reach? The truly developed soul knows that what happens to flesh and blood is irrelevant compared to the destiny of the soul. What matters are our responses to what happens. Do we see trials as a chance to let go of self? May we not set up these things just to "go for it"? We can't fall on our faces when we really, really try. We gain something just for the effort, no matter what the outcome.

Where is it written that every person with an illness has an attitude problem?

Our friend Joey didn't have an attitude problem. He died of cancer trying to save his wife from hers. When Joey first learned of Ellie's diagnosis, he said over and over, "If I just could take it on myself. . . ." Well, he did. Now, twelve years later, Joey is gone but Ellie is still alive.

Joey personified, "Greater love hath no man than to lay down his life for a friend."

Another friend, Joan, taught us as we watched her live with cancer, more than we ever could have known without her. The disease killed her body, but not her spirit. Faith? You bet, but in what?

Joan and Joey didn't have faith that their bodies should not die, but that their souls should live. Their spirits live on in our memories whenever we feel burdened. If any healing needed doing in their souls before they died, it was done; and through them, healings occurred in all who loved them.

Cayce gave a reading for a woman whose mind, he said, was attuned, her soul was in "at-onement," but her physical condition was a stumbling block. He said she could, like the Son, turn stumbling stones into stepping stones.

Grandma never heard of karma, but those who have and who dismiss illness as karmic justice are inviting the universal law of attraction. Though in some cases the universal law of cause and effect or karma may come into play, the other side of the karma coin is grace. If you're caught in karma, turn over the coin. Take pity on those who arrogantly judge. My heart cries not for those who are sick nearly so much as those who pretend to understand what sickness is, and shrug off the suffering of others as though it were of no concern.

Miracles, or the equivalent, do occur, of course, and regularly. I saw them happen at Grandma's church. Prayer for the sick invokes the Holy Spirit, the soul of the Christ. Healing takes place *always* when the individual involved surrenders to Christ's soul. However, that does not mean the healing is visible physically. It may be, but it isn't necessary to witness ''miracles'' to believe healing has occurred.

The problem of believing as Grandma did—that not being healed is a lack of faith—is that the one who's hurting also feels guilty and unworthy. That's patient-bashing at its cruelest. When God didn't heal Grandma's poor circulation and she lost her leg, she felt she was being punished for not having enough faith. She suffered the pain of gangrene weeks longer than her frustrated doctors thought was possible, trying to muster up one more ounce of faith, sure that God would heal her leg. The sad result was that when it didn't happen the way she'd been taught it should, her mind and spirit were broken in the process.

Grandma couldn't let go of her teachings, or her leg, and we lost her without ever knowing the best of her.

Wherever you are in that mind of yours, Grandma, I hope you're reading this. I love you. Remember when I was little, how I loved to tell secrets? Well, this chapter is for you.

Destiny, elusive and obscure, whisper
for this rendezvous your sweet secrets.

"Destiny lies in what we do about
what we know."
Edgar Cayce Reading
—262-78

13

Secrets of Destiny

The question that always comes to mind about destiny is
whether it is predetermined. According to Cayce, the answer is resoundingly *no*.

We have free will. We participate in our destiny. Our
choices have inevitable, even predetermined results, but
which choices we have made or will make have not been
and are not now predetermined.

Picture a row of paint buckets, each filled with a different
color—red, blue, yellow, green, black, and white. If you
choose to mix the red paint with the blue paint, universal
law has predetermined the result will be purple paint.

Unless you want purple paint, don't mix red with blue.

That's all there is to destiny.

14

Secrets of the
Inner-world Rebels

Once upon a time there was a kingdom populated by many people, some good and some bad. This kingdom had no king, it thought, so every day one of the inhabitants of the kingdom would declare himself king. And every day the inhabitants would bow down to whomever had declared himself king, and the next morning when they arose, they would ask, "Well, who shall be king today?"

Sometimes the one who was king yesterday wanted to be king always, so the inhabitants of the kingdom would go along for a while, just to see if this one was worthy. But pretty soon, the one who would be king would do something stupid and the inhabitants would run amok and refuse to bow down, until someone else was king. This went on for quite some time until one of the wise ones said, "You know, we need a real king—one who is worthy of the job, one we can trust." They searched and searched, but none in the kingdom seemed worthy.

Like all good kingdoms, this one had a tower, where locked away was a man no one had thought about for a long time. The inhabitants of the kingdom had forgotten he was there. No one could even remember how he got there.

Then one day a tower guard paid a call on one of the wise ones and said, "Wise one, there is something strange about this man in the tower. He never ages, he never changes, he never asks for anything. He just sits there, patiently smiling. He's always kind to me whenever I see him, so I asked him why he was smiling and he told me this: 'I am smiling because my subjects have never been able to replace me as king. This is my kingdom, and these are all my children. I have remained in this tower so that they might seek among themselves for a king. When I take the throne I want them all to know who I am. I want them to come to me on their own to claim their inheritance.

"'You see, there is wealth beyond their wildest dreams, and only I know where it is hidden. I placed it there long ago, waiting for my children to seek me out, to remember where I let them put me long ago, in this tower where I have been for so long they have forgotten.

"'Once, they knew me. We played together among the stars and laughed and sang as friends. But I loved them too much to keep them there. I wanted them to know the joy of fathering their own creations. I made them sleep for a very long time, and when they awoke, they couldn't remember who they were. I came to them and said, "I am your Father." But they didn't believe me and locked me away in this tower. And here I have remained, hoping that someday I will have the love of at least some of my children back again. I could have bought their love with my wealth, but I want them to claim it as their birthright, not accept it as dole. I do not bribe my children.'"

The wise one listened attentively to the tower guard. The guard's story seemed to awaken in the wise one some memory of once having laughed and played among the stars. The wise one conferred with the other wise ones, and they, too, seemed to recall such a time. Soon word spread among the inhabitants of the kingdom that in the tower was a man who promised great wealth. The rumors flew back and forth while each one searched his memory for the time when they played among the stars.

One said, "I don't really remember, but I'm tired of wondering who shall be king today? Let's give him a try."

Another said, "I don't remember either, but I'm tired of being poor. Let's give him a try."

But one rebelled and said, "No. I want to be king myself. I don't want another."

"What can you offer us?" they asked him.

"Well, I'm pretty smart. I'll figure something out."

"Not good enough," they said. "We'll never bow down to you. We're all pretty smart ourselves. That's not enough. We need someone to take charge of this kingdom so we can be about our business."

The rebel who would be king was angry, but outnumbered. He pretended to submit, but began plotting his strategy to gain control of the kingdom.

A wise one, standing alongside the tower guard listening, said, "The man in the tower says that he is your father and this is his kingdom."

"Fine," they said. "If this is his kingdom, then everything about it concerns him, even what we do."

"That is true," said the wise one.

"So that means our business is his business," they said.

"That is what it means," said the wise one.

They conferred among themselves for a moment, then turned to the tower and said, "Release our father from the tower. We shall put him on the throne and be about his business. From now on we shall know *who shall be king today*."

The kingdom in this fable is, of course, the human mind—its inhabitants, aspects of mind, habits, and inner-world rebels. Doubtlessly, if this tale continued, the rebel would gather his friends, battle for the kingdom, and try to overthrow the king. These rebels are the aspects of mind who refuse to acknowledge the father as king or the king as father. It's hard to fathom why they would not when their share of the wealth is so great. But since the beginning the battle for the kingdom has been fought within the human mind. And since whatever is in the mind manifests in the outer world, wars of one type or another never cease.

The battles are fought first within ourselves, then outside of ourselves. Habits are inner-world rebels who would be king. Habits try to enslave us and often succeed. Which habits are worthy of being king—even for a day? Even good habits—routines into which we slide and become trapped—are unworthy of ruling the kingdom. The mind set about the father's business bows down to no such ruler.

Once we identify who shall be king today, we are *free* to go about our business in complete *faith* that each task is of concern to the father. Each inhabitant, each aspect of mind, is a child of the king—be they rebels or not.

Throughout the kingdom are little pockets of rebeldom where the insurrectionists rise against authority. Much mental energy can be expended quelling the mutiny unless these rebels are transformed into cooperative citizens of the realm. Suppressing the rebels and locking them in the tower won't change them, only make them more determined to take over. Reasoning with these rebels will do little good either. They must voluntarily surrender to rehabilitation. They must be rounded up and brought before the king and left there. The king who is their father will deal with them in his own good time. Meanwhile, don't let them interfere with the business at hand.

Though few remember playing among the stars, a sense of rightness resonates about the idea of the Creator loving the creation enough to want us to experience the joy of creating. That kind of love resounds in our desires for our own earthly children, who sometimes rebel, too. The satisfaction a parent feels when seeing a child get a sense of itself exemplifies how the Creator must feel when we begin to get a sense of ourselves as creators. Yet with the Father it goes beyond mere creating. With Him on the throne, we begin to co-create with Him, and therein lies the business at hand.

We were created to leave the Creator, then return to the Creator better than we started, that we might become spiritually mature companions with Him.

This is fairly easy to comprehend deep within the soul's mind, but how do we bring it out into the open? How do we experience mind as the kingdom with the king in His rightful place on the throne in our everyday lives? How do we quell the rebellion and claim our inheritance in all situations and circumstances? It happens day by day, in varying degrees, during lucid moments of awareness.

The Edgar Cayce readings advise prayer as a method by which this occurs. The Lord's Prayer is recommended as being particularly effective in awakening us to the awareness of the soul's purpose. The following model might prove helpful in visualizing the location of the King's Throne. The Lord's Prayer follows with an interpretation from the perspective of the fable for the purpose of bringing the meaning behind the words of the prayer into clearer focus.

The king's throne sits at the center of the soul's mind.

Mind Is the Kingdom

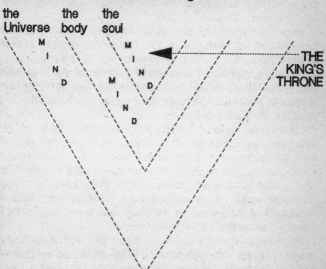

The Lord's Prayer interpreted from the perspective of the fable:

Our Father	O' King, in the
Who are in heaven	kingdom of my mind
Hallowed be Thy Name	I bow down
Thy kingdom come	to your mind
Thy will be done in earth	in my body
As it is in Heaven	as well as my mind.
Give us this day our daily bread	I claim my inheritance.
And forgive us our debts	Pardon my error
as we forgive our debtors.	with justice.
Lead us not into temptation	I will follow you.
But deliver us from evil	Transform the rebels.
For thine is the kingdom	My mind is your mind.
The power and the glory	Lead me home.
Amen.	It is done.

The prayer's effectiveness is enhanced when used as an

affirmation for meditation. Information about how the prayer moves energy throughout the body is included in Chapter 16, "Secrets of Jesus."

With the use of the prayer, an awakening may occur in the memory of being with the Divine in another place, another time. Cayce said, however, not to seek mystical experiences, but to be a mystical experience for someone else. Regardless, though, of what begins to happen or not happen in your life, the inner insurrection can be quelled by bringing the rebels before the king.

Identify the areas of poverty and enslavement in your life that have been built by some aspect of mind. The prayer activates and quickens the soul which then "transmits instructions" to the physical mind from the soul's mind and soul. When or if doubt, mockery, and disbelief arise, these are inner-world rebels making their presence felt. Round them up and take them to the King and leave them there. Then be about the Father's business.

Everything you do throughout the day is the Father's business. Look for opportunities to co-create: be an instrument of peace in the workplace; volunteer to plant a tree; hug your child. Anything that fosters life is co-creative.

As you move through your day, resist the urge to pretend to be poverty-stricken just to fit in with the crowd. You are the child of a king. When faced by outer-world rebels, quietly reaffirm who shall be king today, then take the rebels before the King in prayer and leave them there. Be an instrument of co-creation with the King who wants all rebels to claim their inheritance willingly and acknowledge Him as Father.

"Most of us operate from a narrower frame of reference than that of which we are capable, failing to transcend the influence of our particular culture, our particular set of parents, and our particular childhood experience upon our understanding. It is no wonder, then, that the world of humanity is so full of conflict."

—M. Scott Peck
The Road Less Traveled

15

Secrets of the Bible

The secrets of the Bible are not the province of religion, but of each individual human mind and soul. The Bible belongs to each one of us as personal instruction in thinking, acting, being. Edgar Cayce read the Bible sixty-seven times—once for each year of his life—and insisted that everything we need to know; indeed, more than we shall ever comprehend about "spirituality," is in there.

Comprehension comes with the willingness to read it from our own perspective.

I heard a self-proclaimed religious leader say publicly, "More power to you who speak King James English." She said she herself preferred one of the simpler versions, such as The Living Bible. Without intending to be amusing, she was right about King James: "More power to you." The power comes from the new depths of understanding that are reached through discovering the secrets in the Bible, regardless which version.

There are two routes to the discovery: one is quicker and shorter, less tedious, but less satisfying. It is, however, better than staying in the same old place. All the luggage required is your own interpretation of the words.

As merely a suggestion to stimulate thinking: the Bible becomes clearer if you picture Jesus as the Christ Mind speaking and moving through the cities and villages of your own mind. Picture every person spoken to—even if unrecognizable—as an aspect of your whole human mind. The disciples, the lepers, the blind, the dumb, the lame, the centurion, and the centurion's servant all represent different phases, states, consciousnesses, each with its own thoughts and ideas, some healthy, some not. Try to get a sense of all the people in the Bible as representative of thoughts and ideas that we have fathered, or that have fathered us.

Picture the Bible's ships as vessels: your body and soul body; see the sea and the waters as the unfathomable depths of each human mind, the sea's great storms and tempests mental turmoil.

View the tombs as recesses in the mind, the devils and demons as wrong thoughts and ideas. "The Prince of Devils" deserves special consideration as a particularly strong aspect of mind, as does Satan.

Servants, as well as devils and spirits, can represent ideas also, and often need healing. However, discern in the word "servant" whether it means an idea or thought, a spirit or spirits, or The Spirit, the servant of the Creator.

As an example, here is a quick trip through Matthew 8, sans verse numbers for easier reading, with suggested interpretations and comments in parentheses:

Matthew 8

When he (the Christ Mind) was come down from the mountain, great multitudes (many consciousnesses) followed him. And behold, there came a leper (a diseased aspect of mind) and worshiped him, saying, Lord, if thou wilt (the disease acknowledges His power), thou canst make me clean.

And Jesus (the Christ Mind) put forth his hand and touched him, saying, "I will: be thou clean." And immediately his leprosy was cleansed. And Jesus (the Christ Mind) saith unto him (the newly healed aspect of mind), "See thou tell no man, but go thy way, show thyself to the priest, and offer the gift that Moses commanded for a testimony unto them." (Don't talk about it—then three verbs: go, show, and offer. Act differently. Aspects of mind *act* often as though they are independent. The priest is an aspect of mind in authority.)

And when Jesus (the Christ Mind) was entered into Capernaum (a place of consciousness) there came unto him a centurion (an aspect of mind wise enough to call on the Christ Mind) beseeching him. And saying, "Lord, my servant (an idea) lieth at home sick of the palsy, grievously tormented (a palsied tormented aspect of the centurion)."

And Jesus (the Christ Mind) saith unto him, "I will come and heal him."

The centurion answered and said, "Lord, I am not worthy that thou shouldest come under my roof (into my life): but speak the word only (acknowledges the power of the Christ Mind) and my servant (an idea) shall be healed. For I am a man under authority (other parts of this mind are ruling me), having soldiers (other servants/ ideas) under me: and I say to this man, 'Go,' and he goeth; and to another, 'Come,' and he cometh; and to my servant, 'Do this,' and he doeth it." (This aspect of mind is accustomed to keeping its ideas in line and is befuddled because this one is sick.)

When Jesus (the Christ Mind) heard it, he marveled, and

said to them that followed (other aspects of mind standing around listening), "Verily I say unto you, I have not found so great faith (the Centurion admitted he needed help), no, not in Israel (Israel is souldom). And I say unto you that many (ideas/thoughts) shall come from the east (the light) and west (the soul) and shall sit down with (be with) Abraham, and Isaac, and Jacob (other aspects of mind from the Old Testament), in the kingdom of heaven (a state of mind). But the children (thoughts/ideas) of the kingdom (a state of mind) shall be cast out (discarded) into outer darkness: there shall be weeping and gnashing of teeth." (Old ideas die hard.)

And Jesus (the Christ Mind) said to the centurion (an aspect of mind), "Go thy way; and as thou hast believed, so be it done unto thee." And his servant was healed in the selfsame hour.

And when Jesus (the Christ Mind) was come into Peter's house (the dwelling of a disciple of the Christ Mind), he saw his wife's mother laid, and sick of a fever (Peter's wife, the feminine nature of this aspect of mind, for each aspect of mind as a disciple of the Christ Mind displays traits of both genders). And he (the Christ Mind) touched her hand, and the fever left her: and she arose, and ministered unto them. (The mother of Peter's feminine nature was healed and she resumed her ministering role, which means helping them—all who reside where Peter dwells—to function.)

When the even (evening) was come, they (other aspects of mind) brought unto him (the Christ Mind) many that were possessed with devils (aspects of mind obsessed with wrong thoughts and ideas): and he cast out spirits (discarded the ideas) with his word (the Christ Mind's all-powerful way of insightful speech) and healed all that were sick: that it might be fulfilled which was spoken by Isaiah the prophet, saying, "Himself took (holds up) our infirmities, and bared (exposes them for what they are) our sick-nesses."

Now when Jesus (the Christ Mind) saw great multitudes

(random, meaningless thoughts) about him, he commanded them to depart unto the other side (where it is a little quieter). And a certain scribe (another aspect of mind) said unto him, "Master, I will follow thee whithersoever thou goest."

And Jesus (the Christ Mind) saith unto him, "The foxes have holes, and the birds of the air have nests; but the Son of man hath not where to lay his head." (The Christ Mind was warning that following Him can get a bit uncomfortable.)

And another of his disciples said unto him, "Lord, suffer me first to go and bury my father (an idea that had fathered him, the aspect of mind that followed the Christ Mind). But Jesus (the Christ Mind) said unto him, "Follow me; and let the dead (ideas) bury the dead (ideas)."

And when he (the Christ Mind) was entered into a ship (a human vessel), his disciples followed him (the aspects of mind that follow the Christ Mind). And behold, there arose a great tempest (mental turmoil) in the sea (the mind), insomuch that the ship (the vessel) was covered (overcome) with the waves (perhaps of indecision or other conflicts) and he (the Christ Mind) was asleep. (The Christ Mind sometimes sleeps in some human vessels, and must be awakened. This vessel, as you and I, represents how even when the Christ Mind and the disciples are present, turmoil within the mind can occur. But the Christ Mind is not afraid of turmoil. Read on.)

And his disciples (aspects of mind that follow the Christ) came to him and woke him, saying, "Lord, save us: we perish." (Even disciples become afraid.)

And he saith unto them (the aspects of mind that follow the Christ), "Why are ye fearful, O ye of little faith?" (What is all the fuss about!)

Then (only when asked) he (the Christ Mind) arose, and rebuked the winds and the sea; and there was a great calm (in the mind).

The men marveled (even the disciples could hardly believe it, as we say, "Oh my God, I don't believe it!" when we feel His power), saying, "What manner of man is this, that even the winds and the sea obey him!"

And when he was come to the other side, into the country of Gergesenes (another place in consciousness), there met him two possessed of devils (two aspects of mind obsessed with wrong thoughts and ideas came to meet the Christ mind) coming out of tombs (recesses in the mind), exceedingly fierce, so that no man (no idea) might pass that way (can get by them).

And behold, they cried out, saying, "What have we to do with thee, Jesus, thou Son of God?" (Indicating even the fiercest demons know who He is.) "Art thou come hither to torment us before the time?" (They know their days are numbered.)

And there was a good way off from them a herd of many swine feeding (a herd of thoughts feeding off what swine feed off of—indelicately known as slop). So the devils besought him, saying, "If thou cast us out, suffer us to go away into the herd of swine." (The thoughts don't even try to resist the power of the Christ Mind. They know it is futile. They just try to live a bit longer by becoming a part of other thoughts that are feeding off slop anyway, so who will notice?)

And he (the Christ Mind) simply said, "Go." (One word is sufficient.) And when they (the thoughts) were come out, they went into the herd of swine: and behold (surprise! surprise!), the whole herd of swine ran violently down a steep place into the sea, and perished in the waters (the unfathomable depths of the human mind).

And they that kept them (those aspects of mind that make it possible for those particular devils to live) fled, and went their ways into the city (another place of consciousness) and told everything (warned) and what was befallen (what would happen) to the possessed of the devils. (Note that it says "the possessed of the devils," *the possessed* meaning aspects of mind possessed or obsessed, indicating some portions but not others of the mind can be involved.)

And behold, the whole city (another place in consciousness) came out to meet Jesus (the Christ Mind); and when they saw him, they besought him that he would depart out of their coasts (they rejected him).

Journey into Consciousness

Cayce's concept of "mind as a stream" directs the second, more tedious but more fulfilling route to the discovery of Biblical secrets. Required as luggage: a concordance which includes an original Hebrew, Chaldean, and Greek languages dictionary; and the awareness that today computers are retranslating the translations. Some knowledge of the Bible's checkered history is useful:

The numerous and various shifts and changes in translation are understandable in view of the facts that Hebrew then was written without any spaces separating the words, and that the Hebrew alphabet consisted of twenty-two letters, all of them consonants. Four of the consonants were used to represent vowels, but in writing, only the consonants were put down. It was left up to the reader to insert the proper vowels. As though this were not enough to confuse the issue, often the translators did not agree on which vowels were correct.

This easily raises a question—one that shall not be answered here: is there evidence of the existence of Atlantis in the Bible?

Cayce spoke of the land of Oz; the Bible tells of the land of Uz. The sons and daughters of Belial are spoken of both in the Cayce readings on Atlantis and the Bible. With no vowels in the original manuscripts, who can now say?

Browsing through a concordance often raises other questions. For example, how did Lucifer become a name for evil? Lucifer is only mentioned once in the entire Bible, in

Isaiah 14:12: "How art thou fallen from heaven, O Lucifer, son of the morning! How art thou cut down to the ground, which didst weaken the nations!"

Lucifer comes from *Heylel*, which means "morning star."

Heylel comes from *halal*, which means "to be clear (originally of sound, but usually of color); to shine; hence to make a show, to boast; and thus to be (clamorously) foolish; to rave," etc.

Somehow Lucifer went from being a possibly boastful and foolish but shining morning star to being a "proud, rebellious archangel identified with Satan, who fell from heaven," according to the *Random House Dictionary of the English Language*; Lucifer is also a name for the planet Venus when it appears as a morning star.

Be that as it may, the real key to understanding is to keep in mind that in Spirit there is no such thing as time. In the deepest recesses of inner and outer space, time and light are one. Tracking time is a recent pastime. Until the fourteenth century there were no clocks. Sundials notwithstanding, who knew what year it was really? Only God. As God is Spirit, the words of the Bible are to be interpreted in Spirit, not in earthly terms. Things of the earth are but shadows of Spirit:

"For we are strangers before thee, and sojourners, as were all our fathers: our days on the earth are as a shadow, and there is none abiding." —1 Chronicles, 29:15.

". . . come and put your trust in my shadow . . ." —Judges 9:15.

". . . who serve unto the example and shadow of heavenly things . . ." —Hebrew 8:5.

". . . in the shadow of thy wings I will rejoice." —Psalms 63:7.

Be aware that even "shadow" has different connotations than merely being "a dark figure or image cast on the ground or some surface by a body intercepting light," profound though that realization is.

Aesop wrote, "Beware lest you lose the substance by grasping at the shadow."

"Shadow" in scripture comes from one of four Hebrew words, each carrying a slightly different connotation, but each generally relating to shade through the idea of hovering over, phantom, and illusion. The Greek word *skia* translates to "shadow" as "darkness of error" or "adumbration." Random House defines "adumbration" as "a faint image or resemblance of" something.

So, as strangers we sojourn through darkness of error as a faint image or resemblance of truth, afraid to come out of the shadows into the light.

Why?

Why did Horace write: "We are but dust and shadow."?

How did we get this way?

Does the Bible tell us?

Can we learn the secret truths about ourselves by studying scripture?

Do we really want to know?

Even so, what good is learning if Aeschylus was right: "He who learns must suffer. And even in our sleep, pain that cannot forget falls drop by drop upon the heart, and in our own despair, against our will, comes wisdom to us by the awful grace of God."

Is it true that, "For in much wisdom is much grief: and he that increaseth knowledge increaseth sorrow," as Ecclesiastes 1:18 claims?

Or does knowledge lead to appreciation?

Thomas Henry Huxley wrote: "To a person uninstructed in natural history, his country or seaside stroll is a walk through a gallery filled with wonderful works of art, nine-tenths of which have their faces turned to the wall."

Does not the history of human consciousness bear study? Can wisdom be found in such study? Or must we stroll this life with our faces turned against the wall. Are we, the created, not art? We must study for knowledge that wisdom might be revealed.

In a dream a voice said, "The secret of Universal Consciousness is revealed, not discovered. You don't find it. It is revealed to you."

Later awake, I asked the voice, "When is it revealed?"

The answer was, "When you've reached the point of comprehending its secrets."

Revelation then, not discovery, is wisdom. And that which we all seek—transformation of human consciousness into universal consciousness—is wisdom revealed.

The historical consciousness of humankind and the secret to transforming consciousness is revealed in the Bible, and is discoverable by tracing the river of Eden.

This is the longer, more arduous, scenic route into the secret dwelling place. It is not easy going. As any experienced traveler will agree, to venture where even angels fear to tread—no angel ever tread into human consciousness—we must abandon what Milton called "ignoble ease and peaceful sloth" and leave the comforts of laziness behind. To experience thrilling adventure is to leave behind also the notion that life is a spectator sport. Discovery is a do-it-yourself project. Wherever the river leads, we must be willing to go. The river reveals her secrets only to those who complete the voyage.

The history of human consciousness flows through scripture like the river flows out of the garden of Eden.

It is summed up in five verses, the first of which is Genesis 2:10: "And a river went out of Eden to water the garden; and from thence it was parted, and became into four heads."

(One river—one flow of consciousness—with four heads: four possible directions.)

Pison

Genesis 2:11: "The name of the first is Pison. . . ."

The first possibility is Pison, which represents one consciousness, one direction. Pison is mentioned only this once in the entire Bible. Pison encompasses "the whole land of Havilah," which is mentioned seven times; as a person, the son of Joktan, who is mentioned six times; once as a brother of Peleg; and also as a place, before you get to Egypt in the direction of Assyria.

The original Hebrew, however, describes Havilah as the name of two or three Eastern regions, also perhaps of two men. However, *Chaviylah*, as it is spelled in Hebrew [the original translators think], likely came from *chuwl* or *chiyl*, which means: "to twist or whirl in a circular or spiral manner; i.e. to dance, to writhe in pain (especially of parturition [which is the process of bringing forth young], or fear; to wait, to pervert: bear, (make to) bring forth, (make to) calve, dance, drive away, fall grievously (with pain), fear, form, great, grieve, (be) grievous, hope, look, make, be in pain, be much (sore) pained, rest, shake, shapen, (be) sorrow(ful), stay, tarry, travail (with pain), tremble, trust, wait carefully (patiently), be wounded."

Pison, spelled *Piyshown* in Hebrew, means dispersive, which comes from *puwsh* which means "to spread; act proudly: grow up, be grown fat, spread selves, be scattered."

Havilah's "father" Joktan, or *Yoqtan*, which means "he will be made little," comes from *qaton*: "to diminish; i.e., be diminutive or of no account; be a (make) small (thing), be not worthy."

Joktan's "brother" Peleg, which means "earthquake," comes from *peleg*, which means "a rill (i.e., a small channel of water, as in irrigation): river stream." And *peleg* comes from *palag*, which means to "split or divide."

Thusly the consciousness of the "family of humankind" began.

However, "there is gold" in the land of Havilah—Genesis 2:11. Gold comes from *zahab*, which comes from an unused root meaning "to shimmer; gold; figuratively, something gold-colored, (i.e., yellow), as oil, a clear sky: gold(en) fair weather."

"And the gold of that land is good: there is bdellium and the onyx stone." —Genesis 1:12.

"Good" in this case comes from *towb*, meaning "good in the widest sense; be, do, go, play well."

"Bdellium" comes from *bdolach*, meaning "something in pieces, i.e., a (fragrant) gum (perhaps amber); others a pearl."

"Bdolach" comes from *badal*, which loosely means "to divide, separate, distinguish, differ, select, etc.; to put asunder, to make separate, to sever out utterly."

"Onyx" was translated from *shoham*, which is from an unused root probably meaning to blanch; a gem, probably the beryl (from its pale green color).

"Stone" was translated from *eben*, meaning "to-build," and *eben* comes from *banah*, which means "to build surely, begin to build, obtain children, make, repair, set up."

"Land" was translated from *erets*, from an unused root "probably meaning to be firm; the earth (at large), common, country, earth, field, ground, land, nations, way, wilderness, world."

Thusly the "family of humankind" began to make its way through the wilderness of choices: grievous, writhing, fearful, painful separation, or clear skies and fair weather.

Gihon

Next comes Gihon that circles the land of Ethiopia. —Genesis 2:13.

Gihon comes from *Gichown*, which comes from *giyach*, which means "to gush forth (as water), generally to issue: break forth, labor to bring forth, come forth, draw up, take out.

Ethiopia was translated from "Kuwsh, the name of Cush, a son of Ham and his territory." So to understand the consciousness connected with Ethiopia/Cush, described both as a person and a place, as was Havilah, look at Genesis 10:7 and see that Havilah is described as a "son of Cush." But Cush also, in verse eight, "begat Nimrod; he began to be a mighty one in the earth."

Cush/Ethiopia is that consciousness which comes from Ham, which comes from *cham*, meaning "hot; warm; hot from the tropical habitat." *Cham* comes from *chamam*, meaning "to be hot, (literally and figuratively): enflame self, get (have) heat, be (wax) hot, warm." This may account for the error in our perception of hell.

Ham is described in Genesis 9:18 as "the father of Canaan." Canaan comes from *kana*, which means "to bend the knee; to humiliate, vanquish: bring down, (low) into subjection, under, humble, self, subdue."

Nimrod, as the brother of Havilah, would share some of the same traits of pain and grievous suffering, and as the son of Cush/Ethiopia, would perpetuate the consciousness of humiliation and worthlessness.

The beginning of Nimrod's kingdom was Babel. *Babel* means "confusion." Babel comes from *balal*, meaning to "overflow (specifically with oil); by implication to mix; anoint, confound, fade, mingle, mix (self), give provender [fodder for domestic animals], temper. Furthermore, "to mix" comes from *beliyl*, which sounds exactly like Belial, as previously noted, often mentioned in the Bible and the Cayce readings as representing evil.

Babel and Babylon are translated from the identical Hebrew word, *balal*.

Thusly, "Gihon, encompassing the land of Ethiopia" is that which "fathered" the consciousness of confusion, worthlessness, belittlement, pain, and fear, but also hope to be, do, go, and play well; perhaps to find the amber and pearls; perhaps to shimmer just a little, as did Solomon, when he rode David's mule into and was appointed king in Gihon. (See 1 Kings 1: 33-45).[1]

---

[1]See also 2 Chronicles 32:30, where King Hezekiah stopped the upper watercourse of Gihon and prospered in all his works. Then 33:14, where Manasseh built a wall on the west side of Gihon. In some translations, Manasses of Rev. 7:6 and Manasseh are one and the same.

Hiddekel

"And the name of the third river is Hiddekel: that is it which goeth toward the east of Assyria." Genesis 2:14.

The only other time Hiddekel is mentioned is in Daniel 10:4. Daniel had had a vision three weeks prior that revealed something very upsetting. He had eaten "no pleasant bread, nor flesh nor wine," nor had he bathed for twenty-four days when he said, ". . . I was by the side of the great river, which is Hiddekel."

An entity appeared to Daniel to help him interpret his vision. Therefore to be "by the side of the great river" suggests a state of receptive consciousness flowing. But Hiddekel "goeth toward the east of Assyria."

"East" in this case comes from *qidmah*, which is the feminine of *qedmah*, which comes from *qadam*, which means "to project oneself, i.e., precede; hence to anticipate, hasten, meet (usually for help)."

Furthermore, *qedmah* means "the front or place (absolutely the forepart) or time (antiquity); often used adverbially (before, anciently, eastward): aforetime, ancient (time), before, east (end, part, side, -ward), eternal, ever(lasting), forward, old, past."

So Daniel projected himself "eastward," either back into the past, or ahead into the future.

Assyria was translated from *Ashshuwr*, which in one sense comes from *ashar*, which means "to be straight (used in the widest sense, especially to be level, right, happy); figuratively, to go forward, be honest, prosper: (call, be) bless(ed, happy), go guide, lead, relieve. In another sense Assyria comes from *ashur*, which means "a sense of going; a step."

Daniel was so psychic he was "ten times better than all the magicians and astrologers that were in all his realm." —Daniel 1:20.

When King Nebuchadnezzar had a dream that terrified

him so much he forgot it, he ordered Daniel to recall the dream and interpret it, which, of course, Daniel did. It's no small feat to project oneself eastward into Assyria, meet another's dream, and be able to relieve anxiety about it. But that's what Daniel could do because he had the consciousness of Hiddekel. He could pass through the universal door of creation and be in the consciousness flow of Hiddekel.

Euphrates

"And the fourth river is Euphrates." —Genesis 2:14.

The Euphrates is the only river to make it into The Revelation; indeed, the New Testament. Its mysteriousness is enhanced by the description of the original Hebrew, *P(e)rath*, from an unused root meaning "to break forth; rushing; a river of the East."

Then like Hiddekel, Euphrates pertains to projecting consciousness, but what kind of consciousness? For the answer, follow Euphrates into The Revelation.

Revelation 9:13-15: "And the sixth angel sounded, and I heard a voice from the four horns of the golden altar which is before God, saying to the sixth angel, which had the trumpet, "Loose the four angels which are bound in the great river Euphrates." And the four angels were loosed, which were prepared for an hour, and a day, and a month, and a year, for to slay the third part of men."

Then Revelation 16:12: "And the sixth angel poured out his vial upon the great river Euphrates; and the water thereof was dried up, that the way of the kings of the east might be prepared."

In this case, the word "East" was translated from the Greek *anatole*, which means a "rising of light, i.e., dawn (figuratively); by implication the east: dayspring, east, rising."

Anatole springs from *anatello*, meaning "make to rise," which springs from *telos*, then *tello*, which means to "set out for a definite point or goal; the conclusion of an act or state; result (immediate or prophetic); purpose."

"Kings," interestingly, was not translated from the Greek word meaning simply "to rule." Instead, it was translated from *basileus*, meaning "a sovereign through the notion of a foundation of power." Then goes to *basis*, meaning "to walk, a pace, foot."

The joyous conclusion is that "the way of the kings of the east" means those who walk with a definite purpose into the rising of the light.

And that those who walk with purpose into the rising of the light are the kings of the east.

The question, therefore, is: why does the water of the Euphrates have to dry up so that this way can be prepared?

The clues are in water, dried, vial, or angel.

"Water" comes from *hudor* and *huo*, which mean "rain or showers."

"Dried" comes from *xeraino*, which means "to desiccate; by implication, to shrivel up."

So what could be in the angel's vial that could make it stop raining?

"Vial" comes from *phiale*, meaning "broad, shallow cup."

"Angel" is from *aggelos*, "a messenger."

There are "four angels *bound* in the great river Euphrates" to be loosed.

"Bound" comes from *deo*, meaning simply "to be in bonds." But *deo* comes from *deomai*, the middle voice of *deo*, and means "to beg (as binding oneself); i.e., petition: beseech, pray (to) make request."

"Loose" comes from *luo*, meaning "literally or figuratively to break (up), destroy, dissolve, (un)loose, melt, put off."

Now we're getting somewhere.

These four messengers in bondage, begging, beseeching, and praying, are—at the time of revelation—dissolved. The consciousness of bondage, begging, beseeching prayer is to be no more.

They "were prepared to slay the third part of men."

"Prepared" comes from *hetoimazo*, which means "to provide or make ready."

"Slay" is from *apokteino*, which means "to destroy, put to death."

"Third" is from *tritos*, meaning "a third part."

"Part" is from *merizo*, which means "to part; i.e., (literally) to apportion, bestow, share, or (figuratively) to disunite, differ: deal, be difference between, distribute, divide, give part."

Merizo comes from *meros*, which means "to get as a section or allotment."

Therefore, "Loose the four angels which are bound in the great river Euphrates" translates to:

Dissolve, break up, or destroy the four messengers which are in bondage, beseeching, praying, and begging (because they have bound themselves), and who have been making ready to put to death the "tritos," division or apportionment.

Then, "And the sixth angel poured out his vial upon the great river Euphrates; and the water thereof was dried up, that the way of the kings of the east might be prepared..." reads:

So the sixth messenger emptied his broad, shallow cup, and the rain shriveled, so the kings of the east, who walk from a basis of power and with a definite purpose, may walk into the rising of the light.

Therefore, to project the consciousness of the Euphrates is to project the idea that we have been bestowed bondage and separateness. The four messengers want to destroy that idea so that we may know—by immediate or prophetic results—*sovereignty*!

The consciousness of an allotment of bondage and separateness begins in Genesis and ends in The Revelation. The boundaries are now dried up. It is no longer raining. The sky is clear. The light is rising.

Those who will may walk with purpose out of the shadows into that light.

Note: the Euphrates today flows through Turkey, Syria, and Iraq. Is not the conflict in the Middle East but a reflected shadow of our own warring spirits?

16

Secrets of Jesus

The secrets of Jesus are the secrets of each one of us.

Edgar Cayce consistently said that Jesus is the pattern. When you want to make a suit of clothes, unless the pattern and the instructions (the knowledge of how to cut and sew it) are imprinted in your mind, you must have a paper pattern, which someone first had to make. When you want to make a life, Jesus is the pattern imprinted on your soul mind.

Cayce indicated that when we have truly begun to understand the secrets of the universe, the life of Jesus takes on new meaning. He said we must all answer the questions, "What will we do with this man Jesus? What will we do with this man called Christ?"

Jesus is the pattern who comes with a set of instructions: the Bible. Only the Bible, as we've seen, being somewhat like the instructions that come with a put-it-together-yourself computer manufactured in Taiwan, written by someone who doesn't understand English, you might need Divine intervention to comprehend the nuts from the bolts. Most people would just give up, let somebody else assemble the computer, and hope. Only when the computer breaks, you still don't know how to fix it because you don't understand its inner secrets.

Suppose the assembler did know what he was doing. Suppose he knew he was moving and wrote you a new set of instructions in your language. You would still have to read and study to comprehend and follow them.

Suppose, better still, the assembler came to your house and the two of you together wrote the instructions, word for word, part by part. You'd have a little better idea of what those instructions say, and how to use them when needed because you've had some input as to their contents. You've used words you understand. Now you would have some familiarity with what makes that computer hum. Your anxiety level would drop considerably.

But the best written instructions won't help unless you read them. That's why, "when all else fails, *read the instructions*."

When studying the life of the Master in the Bible, in the Cayce readings, or in other comparative studies, realize that you aren't making a suit of clothes or trying to assemble or repair a computer. This is for keeps. Your soul's destiny depends on what you do about the pattern, not what someone else does or says you must do. This is strictly a do-it-yourself project. Because someone else understands or thinks they understand the pattern is not the same as understanding Him yourself. You can listen until your ears fall off to others who think they know. But until you close your ears to others, and listen to Christ's soul, the Comforter, you'll never really know who or what speaks truth. You seek the spirit of truth, not dogma.

Dogma can be like a department store where you pay

your money and make your choice of ready-made garments in the color and style of the season. On the other hand, the spiritual realm is more like a fabric shop, where a lustrous array of beautiful materials await your touch. You may construct the outer garment in which you wish to be seen unconfined by style dictates, or by someone else's notion about how you should look; that is, *if* you can read a pattern and wield a scissor.

If you discover the garment is unacceptable, there's always the department store waiting. It's the easier way. No mess, no fuss, no bother with brain strain, no countless fittings, no stitches to rip out and redo. You may, however, say, "Why am I doing this? The little boutique down the street has exactly what I want!" Congratulations. You just discovered something. You are in harmony with another's ideas about who you are. The garments fit. You look and feel good in them. Of course, you may have that experience in the large department store of religions. The garments that clothe the soul are thoughts constructed by the mind.

Thoughts and ideas may enhance the soul's individuality or drape the soul in such a way that it becomes lost within the folds. There is one idea, however, that is perfect for the soul. That idea is the Ideal. The Ideal is the garment so beautifully tailored that the soul strives always to wear it. That garment is made by the pattern. The pattern was made by The Designer, who placed the instructions in your soul.

The pattern of Jesus discerned from the Edgar Cayce readings is, in part, this: Each experience Jesus had depicts the journey of each soul on its way back to the Father. He existed before the world was, as did we. He experienced many incarnations in the earth, as have we. When He was ready, he became Christed, as will we.

Before He was Jesus who became the Christ, Cayce's story of the Master includes lives as Amelius, Adam, Enoch, Hermes, Melchizedek, Joseph, Joshua, Asaph, Jeshua, and Zend. These lives have been chronicled in *Lives of the Master: The Rest of the Jesus Story*, by Glenn Sanderfur.[1]

[1]A.R.E. Press, 1988.

The Holy Trinity of Father as the body, Christ as the mind, and Spirit as the soul is imprinted in each of us. This is how we know eternal life. Jesus perfected the way.

A look at some of the symbology of Jesus' birth, life, and death through Cayce's eyes may help to understand the significance of Jesus.

The angels heralded the coming of Christ into the earth. Angels are real beings, but they also signify perceptive faculties of Spirit within each of us—faculties that never left heaven to sleep in the earth. These perceptive faculties make us aware of our potential.

The star that appeared in the East, leading the wise men to attend the birth of the Christ into the earth, represents the light that guides us.

The symbology of the East is interesting in that a cherubim, usually thought of as an angel child, though described in the dictionary as an imaginary figure, was placed at the east gate of the Garden of Eden. The source of all life, the sun (the son?) rises in the east, making the east symbolic of enlightenment. A literal and/or imaginary child stands guard at the gate to Paradise, holding a light to help guide us homeward.

The three wise men symbolize the physical, mental, and spiritual aspects of man. When guided by the star, they left their business and sought the Christ.

Shepherds also sought the Christ child. They symbolize our reason and will. Then physical, mental, and spiritual, joined by reason and will, behold the Christ.

Mary, who also entered the earth without a human father, represents our soul, faith incarnated, the mother of power. Power entered the earth through the body of faith, fathered by love. Love and faith created power, the Christ Child, Jesus. Love and faith made possible the first coming of Christ just as love and faith make possible the birth and second coming of Christ within each of us.

Joseph on one level represents our intellect. At first Joseph didn't understand how power could be born of faith and love. But on another level Joseph represents our feminine perceptiveness, demonstrated when an angel, his perceptive faculty, made him aware of his potential as a nurturer and protector of the coming child.

While in Bethlehem to pay taxes—the soul/spiritual and the intellect/mental must give up whatever is required of them in order to be aligned with the law physically—the child was ready to appear.

There was no room in the inn, a place of many states of misunderstanding and confusion. The Christ could not be born in such a place. He had to appear in a setting of simple humility, a stable. There the physical, mental, and spiritual could kneel before Him with their gifts. Reason and will could bow down to Him in acquiescence to His superiority, as we do when we know Him.

Herod symbolizes our fearfulness, our ego, our reluctance to allow the child to live for fear He will take over. But Mary and Joseph moved Him into Egypt, a different place in consciousness, until the death (in Matthew 2:19) of ego, Herod. But Mary/soul and Joseph/intellect parented and loved the child secretly, so that He grew in "wisdom and stature."

(We must use our imaginations to ponder what kind of parents Mary and Joseph were . . . faith as Mary, the loving mother who never fails us; intellect as Joseph, the loving father who helps us understand. There must be a lesson there for us in nurturing our own physical earth children, as well as the Christ child within ourselves.)

As He reached the age of twelve, meaning the five senses and the seven psychic centers are now activated by the Christ principle, He began to teach in the temple, which represents the mind as well as the body of man. When he began to teach, he also began to be taught by the Essenes, as we come under the guidance of special teachers when we are ready. But even then, before he began his public ministry, he spent forty days in the wilderness, symbolic of human temptation, and going within. The number forty, made up of four, perfect balance of heredity, environment, mind, and soul, plus a zero or circle, the cycle without beginning and without end, represents reaching the perfected state.

He emerged purified and strengthened, ready to choose His disciples, which represent the twelve aspects of man's being in the form of love, faith, power, law, imagination, creativity, understanding, reason, judgment, enthusiasm, will, and intuition. The potential Christ of ourselves has these twelve faculties to serve us.

Our Twelve Disciples

Love is God. The whole law is fulfilled in these three words. The Father, seeking to manifest Himself, brought life as we know it into being through love. He gave to us the ability to become one with Him, as Mary did, through faith. The Son was shown the way, and through Him, we can learn the way to be one with love.

Faith is the inner spiritual knowledge of the Creative Forces of the universe. Faith accepts or rejects, as Mary did, without basis of reason, beyond the ken and scope of that which is perceived through the five senses. It is the failure of our senses to perceive and fully to understand the secrets of the universe that causes us to stumble. Faith is necessary to bridge the span between the seen and the unseen.

Power comes from desire that drives our physical and our spiritual self, and true power comes when each struggling soul faces the realities of life by making its desire one with the Father's. Jesus' desire to glorify God gave Him the power to do miracles, as it does us.

Law is of God. Of the many laws at work in the universe, the hardest truth for us to accept is that they are all of God. It is almost impossible to accept the concept of "The Lord Thy God is One." Everything that exists, regardless whether it's perceived as good or evil, is all of the Father. In Him all moves and lives and has its being. There is no other.

Imagination, the faculty of imagining, or of forming mental images or concepts of what is not actually present to the senses, is the forerunner to all creativity. What we think, put our mind to work upon, to live upon, to feed upon, to live with, to abide with—that is what our soul-body becomes.

Jesus showed us how to fulfill our human potential, how to think with the Christ mind. Actually, "Christ mind" is redundant, for Christ *is* mind in the ultimate.

Creativity is inevitable. We cannot *not* create. Our very bodies are composites of creativity manifested in a physical world. When we are attuned to the Creator, we create miracles. Otherwise, our creations can become monsters. Jesus used His power of Christ to create enough food to feed five thousand, then told us we could learn to do likewise.

Understanding is beyond the reason of the senses. It is the power to see, experience, and interpret the laws that govern the expression of creativeness in and through the physical, mental, and spiritual bodies of mankind. An understanding of the mysteries of life comes to those only who dare make a close approach to the Throne.

Reason, as a basis or cause for some belief or act, is developed by learning to see beyond what can be perceived by the unaided, naked eye and by the conscious mind. Reason also is the shepherd that watches over thoughts, represented by sheep, which will follow after one another blindly. As the Good Shepherd watches over his sheep, reason guards our thoughts, attitudes, and emotions.

Judgment, as the ability to form an opinion or make a decision objectively, is analyzing and evaluating the knowledge we have gained. If we are truly to know God in a way that can help someone else, we must just do what we know at the moment, then more will be given. Jesus taught us, his disciples, to observe the fruits of the tree.

Enthusiasm is awareness of God within. "Let others do as they may, but as for us, we will worship—yea, we will serve—the living God."

Will is the origin of desire, the directing force that drives us mentally. Will is closely linked with purpose, which stimulates desires that grow and take hold of the mind as habits take hold of the body. The desire of Jesus by the age of twelve was to "be about the Father's business." As *all that is* is of the one, everything is "the Father's business."

Intuition, the direct perception of truth, facts, and so

forth, immediate apprehension, independent of any reasoning process, is the natural result of "losing self in Him."

Be aware that one or more of these "disciples" has the potential of betrayal and denial, as Judas would betray Jesus and Peter would deny Him so the plan could be carried out.

For the next three years, Jesus and His disciples went about teaching and preaching, demonstrating power. The first miracle He performed, at the urging of his mother, Mary, was to turn water into wine. Symbolically, each of us must heed the urgings of soul and, in faith, transform ourselves as the water was transformed. The miracle occurred at a wedding, a merging of two into one, a consummation of consciousnesses, alone incapable of generation, but together capable of manifesting life into the earth. At the time of the inner marriage, the transmuting power of Christ is called forth.

Jesus was reluctant to demonstrate the power. However, He responded to the urgings of His mother, as Spirit always answers the call of our souls.

The six stone waterpots represent our five senses, plus the sixth, intuitive sense. When touched by the Christ power, the water transformed into a liquid capable of altering the consciousness.

Each succeeding miracle demonstrated that when we fully comprehend "I and my father are one," it is possible to alter the atomic structure of matter, such as when He walked on water, and restored the sick to wholeness. Yet even with such power, He had to complete His mission of human expression by defeating death. At the end, He surrendered. In humility He commended His soul into the hands of the Father. He had insisted all along that He of Himself as a man could do nothing. There on the cross, a symbol of man with his arms outstretched, He let us see that the time comes when it will be just us and God. The earth mind must die before Christ resurrects. But that wasn't the end of it.

The three-day entombment represents our time of going within, to become aware of the new consciousness, to become fixed, so that when the stone is rolled away we can show ourselves anew. The doubter, Thomas, was not there with the other disciples when the resurrected Christ "breathed on them, and said, 'Receive ye the Holy Ghost.' "[2] This is important because it represents how even after we experience the power of Christ within ourselves, some faithless aspect of self, represented by the doubting Thomas, requires more proof, must thrust its hand into His side, before we will believe. Some part of us doesn't trust what we are hearing and seeing. We more or less have to gather all the disciples, all aspects of self, into one room, one place in consciousness, and give them even more signs of the truly risen Christ before we accept it.

Before the crucifixion Jesus was betrayed by Judas, and denied by Peter, just as some aspects of ourselves deny and betray us. We must forgive those parts of ourselves as He forgave them and finish the work we have come to do so that we may ascend to the Father, a risen Christ. After the resurrection, He was doubted and disbelieved, as we doubt and disbelieve He is risen in us.

In Jerusalem, when the disciples were praising Jesus as the "King that cometh in the name of the Lord," the Pharisees, which represent our negative attitudes, asked Him to rebuke the disciples. (But even they called Him Master. See Luke 19:39.) Jesus told the Pharisees that if the disciples should "hold their peace, the stones would immediately cry out,"[3] indicating that all of creation, even nature, knows of Christ, which is why nature serves us in our understanding of Him.

Juliet Brook Ballard began her book, *The Hidden Laws of the Earth*,[4] with this story:

"A most arresting concept was presented to me when I was still a child.

"My aunt and I were looking at a fire on our family hearth. I was basking in the warmth, enjoying the beauty of the ascending flames, but being careful not to go too close and risk being burned.

[2](Luke 20:22.)
[3](Luke 39:40 and Reading 262-45, A.)
[4]*The Hidden Laws of the Earth*, A.R.E. Press, 1979.

" 'You have learned about fire,' my aunt remarked. 'You know that if you put your hand in it, it will burn you. It will burn anyone, even a person who doesn't know any better. The fire does not care whether or not you know.' "

She goes on to say that someday perhaps "science will catch up with Edgar Cayce," that the readings see science and religion as one, in their purpose of discovering the truth. Whether we understand it, the law is at work, and all the laws are God. The law doesn't care whether or not we know, any more than the fire does. It will burn us if we misuse it.

Jesus teaches us how to align with the law, to use it, not misuse it.

It is our blind misuse of law that has created the world in which we live today. As little gods, desiring to express ourselves, we have taken what we don't understand, life, and thrust ourselves into cities and villages of separateness. We've feared and hated creations different from our own. We've tried to wrench the power away from God and have re-created man in our own image. What we in our dark ignorance don't understand, we mistrust.

On one occasion Jesus beheld a city and "wept over it."[5] He said if we only knew the things which belong to us, but are hidden from our eyes, that keep us from peace. . . .

He tried to tell us to tolerate one another's different states of awareness. Instead, we rail against each other's differences, and try to convert one another to this belief or that. We pass on beliefs to our children as they have been passed on to us. But Cayce said our minds, which have the ability to make comparisons, to reason, to have reactions through the senses, can be attuned through the will to re-create our environment, even our hereditary influences. When we take the only thing that is ours, will, and place it at the disposal of the Christ, mind and soul join forces to produce changes physically when we work with the law. We don't have to understand the law, just live by it.

The frustration of thinkers throughout the ages has been

[5](Luke 19:41.)

to understand the mind of God. Cayce said that Jesus, the Son, represents the mind of God, and the only way to know God is to know Jesus. That frustration has produced countless millions of words on the subject. Mind called the Universe into being. In the final analysis, Mind is the motivating force of each atom. As yet we cannot comprehend something that functions without form or body. The question, "Before Mind was, what?" cannot be answered because the concept of nothingness is futile. We can conceive of ourselves as souls without bodies. We can even visualize soul without mind. But there it stops. We can't get beyond mind without mind. Questions such as, "If God created us, who created God?" are intellectual distractions designed to avoid the ultimate reality: We and our world are expressions of the mind of God, the Son. We don't have to know why fire burns. It's enough to use the fact that it does, indeed, burn to reap the benefits or to suffer the consequences. It's our choice.

Cayce's persistence that Jesus exemplified the mind that brought worlds into existence is why he also said, "Call none but He, Master."

How Did He Become the Master?

It's too simple to say He knew Himself to be the Son of God; therefore, He could work miracles. What made Him so special? What did He do that we don't?

It was the way He used His senses. Trying to be like Him without using our physical senses is like trying to blow up half a balloon; it's an exercise in futility.

He projected Himself into a human body with five senses and seven spiritual centers just like ours. As a human, He was working through twelve faculties, as outlined previously, as we do. He had the senses of sight, hearing, taste, touch, and smell. He had the seven chakras that are connected to the pineal, pituitary, thyroid, thymus, adrenals, Leydig cells, and gonads. He worked with seven physical systems, as we do: circulatory, nervous, respiratory, digestive, eliminative, lymphatic, and endocrine. His brain had four lobes and twelve billion neurons, like ours. But He could see things we can't see.

He condemned the Pharisees and the Sadducees for not seeing, for being unable to "discern the signs of the times." The Bible carried hundreds of references to eyes, such as "having eyes see ye not"; "Blessed are the eyes that see"; "Lift up your eyes and look."[6]

There are many references to ears, as well. Approximately a dozen times the Master said, "He that hath an ear, let him hear."

Five of the references to taste mention not tasting death. Hundreds mention eating and drinking.

The Master's apparently favorite way of healing was by touch. He touched and felt if He was touched, even the hem of His garment.

He didn't care to smell burnt offerings; instead, He preferred a sweet-smelling sacrifice. As the crowds pressed in on Him, he could smell the stench of sickness, and He healed as many as asked.

The Master exemplified the opening of the seven centers, which are, according to Cayce, located throughout the endocrine system.

He demonstrated His instinct for survival when He pulled away from the crowds, and again when He prayed for the cup to pass. This instinct is associated with the first chakra, located in the groin or base of the spine.

He demonstrated his emotional nature when He wept, and when He got angry. This nature, associated with the second chakra, located in the lower abdomen, representing the polarity of the masculine and feminine within Himself, was demonstrated by His birth, and then again when He turned the water into wine at the urgings of His mother.

He demonstrated His use of force or power, sometimes called the thinking nature, when He gained His self-awareness at the age of twelve. This nature is associated with the third chakra, located in the solar plexus.

[6](See Matthew 16:3, Mark 8:18, Luke 10:23, John 4:35.)

He demonstrated human love and sympathy, often associated with the reasoning nature, when He blessed the woman at the well. This nature is associated with the fourth chakra, located in the heart or thymus area.

He demonstrated his creative nature when He made the decision to feed the hungry. This nature is associated with the fifth chakra, located in the throat.

He demonstrated His spiritual nature, the higher mind, the integration of the intellect and intuition, or logos, when He knew He would be betrayed. This nature is associated with the sixth chakra, located in the center of the brain.

He demonstrated His Christ nature when He healed the sick. This nature, associated with the seventh chakra, is located behind the forehead.

The five senses and seven centers represent, in Sanskrit tradition, the spokes of a wheel. Each of the twelve spokes extends to a point of contact with the ground of oneself and propels us forward in our understanding of the secrets of Jesus as the Master of the Masters.

The method of prayer suggested by the Master opens the seven spiritual centers in a particular order. "Psychic" ability is the natural result. Each morning the sun reminds us that light dawns slowly. After application, Cayce stressed balance above all else. Otherwise, psychic powers could signify imbalance rather than soul development. In the extreme, imbalance within the spiritual centers or the senses on one or more of the three levels causes symptoms of the mental derangement experienced by psychotics, such as "hearing" voices.

The words of the Lord's Prayer enlighten, awaken, and balance each of the seven centers by spreading energy throughout the physical body:

Our Father which art in Heaven balances the pituitary center, located behind the forehead, also known as the third eye. Associated with the seventh chakra.

Hallowed be Thy Name balances the pineal center, located in the center of the brain. Associated with the sixth chakra.

Thy kingdom come, Thy will be done, on earth as it is in

Heaven balances the thyroid center, located in the throat. Associated with the fifth chakra.

Give us this day our daily bread balances the gonad center, located in the groin area. Associated with the first chakra.

And forgive us our debts as we forgive our debtors balances the adrenal center, located in the solar plexus. Associated with the third chakra.

And lead us not into temptation balances the Leydig cells center, located in the lower abdomen. Associated with the second chakra.

But deliver us from evil balances the thymus center, also known as the immune system, located in the heart area. Associated with the fourth chakra.

For thine is the kingdom returns the energy to the thyroid center.

And the power returns the energy to the pineal center.

And the glory forever. Amen. returns the energy to the pituitary center.

Jesus was telling us that to do as He did, we must possess the power He did. The prayer awakens, enlightens, and balances the secret power that is our natural heritage as brothers and sisters of the Son of God.

17

Secrets of Prophecy

We're fast becoming a planet of prophets. Those guys in the Old Testament had nothing on us. The burning bush was kid stuff compared to talk show channelers. Heck, Moses only channeled God. Today, we have Ramtha. But it's part of our reality—we are *all* psychic, to some degree—so best that we understand something about how prophecy works. And doesn't work.

There is accurate prophecy. That's when the soul mind joins with the soul's soul, and imagination takes the form of memories of the future. That's what precognitive visions *are*.

At the level of the soul's soul, there is no time. Therefore, with time out of the way as a limitation, the soul's mind connects with the soul's soul, taps into the Infinite, so to speak, makes the quantum leap into Infinity, then charges back through the barrier of the subconscious—which knows only the present, not the past and future—and presents information.

Then there's inaccurate prophecy.

If the barrier of the subconscious is not cleared completely, the visions get mangled and become blurred and/or inaccurate. But this mangling occurs at a level unperceived by the conscious mind; therefore, unaware of all the operatives, the conscious mind accepts the illusion, which masquerades as prophecy.

Even Cayce had his problems. When he gave a reading, a "director" asked the questions Cayce should answer. Cayce said if the mind of the person directing a reading was "wishy-washy, willy-nilly," the same could be expected of the information derived. He said the subconscious mind reflects distorted images in the same way a "mirror may be waved or bended to reflect in an obtuse manner. . . ." He said the suggestion itself may "bend the reflection of that given; (but) the image itself is what is reflected and not that of some other."

The secret to prophecy lies in how we perceive ourselves in the distorted self-images the subconscious may, like carnival mirrors, reflect. These self-perception problems commonly urge us to ask, like the wicked queen, "Mirror, Mirror, on the wall, who's the fairest of them all?" The subconscious "mirror" will most often tell us what we want to hear. The universal law of self-preservation may impel the subconscious to lie.

During a reading Cayce experienced an unpleasant, "extraordinary physical reaction," caused, he said, by "the seeking of irrelevant questions." Later he said each one present during a reading should seek the protection of the Christ Consciousness; that each should lay aside the conscious self and "enter in communication with the highest that may be attained in self. *And those who cannot conform should not be present.*"

So much for channeling on talk shows.

It is consciousness of self that gets in the way of the would-be visionary. Self is always the problem.

Self blocks the path of many who would seek to prophesy through dangerous explorations of what Edgar Cayce's son, Hugh Lynn Cayce, called in his book, *Venture Inward*, "automatisms such as the Ouija board or planchette, automatic writing, the pendulum, the dowsing rod," and other gimmicks.

He wrote: "Many people undertake explorations of their own or others' unconscious minds with no thought of preparation, with no understanding of the 'forces' with which they must deal. The jungles of Yucatan are well-marked city streets by comparison. The results of such thoughtless undertakings can be tragic.

"Almost anyone, with a little practice, can get a pencil to write, apparently without consciously moving it. Or it is possible to sit with some friend or relative with fingers lightly touching the top of the little three-legged table (Ouija) and find that it will move from letter to letter, spelling out some message which both persons will swear did not come from their conscious minds.

"The information that generally comes through is just about what would be expected from a subconscious mind into which all kinds of thoughts have been pushed and suppressed. The product of such efforts can be a bewildering blend of nonsense, filth, and homespun philosophy. Fortunately, in most instances, the result is weariness and impatience and the discovery that the unconscious layer available through such techniques is of little help and frequently exceedingly dull.

"The subconscious is quite willing to fool the conscious in order to gain authority and recognition." (pp. 127-128)

The late Gina Cerminara, author of *Many Mansions, World Within,* and other books, placed *Venture Inward* high on the required reading list for people interested in *all* psychic matters, including prophecy.

Hugh Lynn Cayce peered out over an audience one night and said, "People, the subconscious mind is a garbage pit."

His father was more tactful. He usually referred to the subconscious as a storehouse.

They were, of course, both right.

Because it is a storehouse, the subconscious mind may be maintained neatly or become like a garbage dump, where trash lies lingering, festering, and rotting. Without light and air, if left alone, this mess will build sufficient heat and energy to take on a life of its own. It will be smelled for miles around, disgusting and offending those within sight and stench of it. In humans, this garbage dump comes equipped with another feature: it has a mouth. It speaks. Obscene lies thinly veiled by a touch of truth here and there are its forte.

At its worst, a foul, grossly loathsome, noisome bother, a vexation to its own spirit, it may be clogged and obstructed with matter—abominable, wicked, and vile. It may abound in error, encrusted with barnacles like the underwater hull of a ship. As a mooring place it is, when swinging with the tide, fraught with the danger of colliding with other vessels. When the bottom of a body of water is fouled it affords a poor hold for an anchor. The subconscious so easily becomes entangled, bringing dishonor, disgrace, and shame.

However, like a garbage dump or the waters around a marina, the subconscious is not responsible for what it contains. It is a receptor, incapable of managing its own self. The responsibility for itself lies outside of itself. The garbage in the subconscious mainly gets dumped there by the conscious mind.

The history of mankind could be traced through garbage. Matter deteriorates but leaves evidence of its prior existence behind. Analysis of the evidence tells a story. In the subconscious this evidence is memory. Under threat of annihilation by its own garbage, mankind is learning to manage it. One of the techniques used is to turn it often, exposing the waste products to sun and air, rendering them incapable of building their own heat and energy. Occasional purging by fire is another technique used. In the subconscious this turning, burning, and purging is necessary even in a well-managed life.

A well-managed repository of waste—nowadays, they call them landfills—reminds us of our humanness. (And who hasn't poked around in a dump and found a treasure?) Disposal is necessary. If we didn't dump the garbage in our homes, pretty soon we'd be ceiling deep in it. Some garbage goes out regularly; we recognize it instantly for what it is. Some, however, builds up in our closets, until there's no room for the good stuff. Most of us then clean out and start over. I had an uncle who didn't. When he died, the rooms of his tiny little house were no more than pathways lined with stacks of newspapers and junk. He left barely enough room to maneuver; even the doors and windows were blocked, except one of each. He just never did get around to sorting it all out. Which of us does not live to some degree as a human garbage dump?

Sort it all out we must, whether prophesying is the aim or not.

The daily media barrage of garbage mostly gets recognized instantly for what it is. However, some gets accumulated and stacked in a corner, like uncle's papers, for who knows what reason. We surely at some level must know we'll never get around to utilizing that information, so why do we keep it? Likewise for junk mail. Good grief! Throw it out. But how about ideas as junk? That's the stuff we stick in our mental closets, afraid it might have value. Or maybe it once had value, but now we've outgrown it, or it has gone out of fashion. Ideas, like hemlines, rise and fall. So how do you recognize the good stuff that won't go out of style? Go back to the basics.

How?

If you are living in a garbage dump, remember, "God is not the author of confusion. . . ."[1] (I just took a look around my office. There will be a short pause while I tidy up.)

Were it but that simple.

If we all mentally "clean up our act," learn to turn and burn on our own, we will all be prophets, and an entire community of professionals will be out of work. The psychiatrists and psychologists—don't fire them yet; think of them as waste management engineers or an internal janitorial service—get paid for poking around in our individual junk heaps. Often we need their help, first in seeing ourselves, then in deciding what to keep and what to pitch. But when they are no better at sorting their own piles than we are at sorting ours, it becomes a case of the blind leading the blind—better than stumbling alone in the dark, but just barely. Poking around doesn't accomplish the same as turning and burning.

No shrink-basher, I speak personally. Analysis has been helpful when I've been so buried in my own garbage I couldn't breathe. Enough poking allows light and air to reach inside somewhat. If asked I'd say shrink not from shrinks. Take help from whence it comes and all that. But if you aren't seriously disturbed, but only dancing around the edges of the lunatic fringe, like most of us, here's a better way.

1. Stop believing everything you hear. A monstrous lie being foisted upon the spiritual seeker today is: All you have to do is look within and everything will be just dandy.

Watch out for those words; look within is not *all* you have to do. It is the universal law of grace and mercy that dictates there be more to it. Without the other steps, if we could really see when we looked within, we'd be even worse off. If we could see, could remember, could perceive the horrors

---

[1](1 Corinthians 14:33.)

we have wrought, not only would the shrinks be swamped, but the priesthood might get a little crowded, too.

I can hear the news tease now:

Masses wearing sackcloth and ashes weep and wail in the streets. Film at eleven.

Beware, too, of people pushing books written—they say—in a flash of insight. Flashes of insight have a tendency to blind. It's the slow, steady rising of the light that illuminates the landscape—each morning of your life. The very ones who shout the loudest—even if not audibly, but through brassy arrogance—are the ones most likely being blinded by their own glitter, not the light of God.

(Father, protect us from noisome bothers, vexations of spirit, tinkling cymbals. If they shall not be silenced, reveal to us their motives for claiming to love us, but who would enslave us into creeds and dogma not of Your making. At the very least, Father, suffer us not to listen. May we ever be so closely walking in Your shadow, they dare not come close enough to snatch us from your care. Selah.)

Sorry, but despite recent reports to the contrary, we are not—in our present form—perfect or invulnerable. We are not God. We are not even one *with* God except at the soul-of-the-soul level. The potential for being is not the same as being. If we could live in a perfected state of oneness with the Divine, we wouldn't be here.

2. Start believing some of the things you hear. The universal law of truth is at work in the earth, revealing your own glorious, wondrous, imperfect majesty. Yes, you can prophesy. All the answers are within. Yes, look within, but not only at images coming from the subconscious, or you'll miss the best of you. Yes, listen. Please listen, but for silence, not voices. Hearing silence takes work. The still, small voice shouts only in emergencies. The rest of the time it whispers, and you must cut through the clatter in your head to hear it. The clatter is coming from the energy built up in the subconscious. Repressing this energy is not the answer. The clatter and chatter is part of who you are. Own it, love it, ask it to wait its turn. Don't insist, persist.

It's simple, but not easy. Inner power grows, like all great things, slowly. The paradox is that once the power is felt it must be surrendered. Again, simple but difficult. Who wants to give away power? Oh, it is yours to keep if you choose. But you'll never prophesy accurately if you do. Surrender to the Infinite is the secret to prophecy.

The soul-of-your-soul is where you are one with God, everyone and everything else. Touch that and be transformed. Sort of. Here's what I mean by that:

Touching the soul-of-your-soul is transforming, but it does not happen only once and that's that. It happens again and again, each time almost as though it happens thought by thought, attitude by attitude, emotion by emotion, day by day. But we are not faced with only one thought, attitude, and emotion per day. Through the universal law of attraction, we deal daily with many things on many levels. That's why persistent patience is the process rather than a goal.

Each time the transforming touch is accomplished, behavioral changes follow. That's the test. No behavioral change, no transformation. In one situation after another courage replaces cowardice, management replaces manipulation, agreement replaces argument, and so on. It is a lifelong process.

3. Evoke the universal law of expectancy. Start believing everything you hear is for your benefit. *It is*, you know. Not to swallow whole without question, but to examine, to turn over in your mind, to ponder, to test, to see how it fits. You are so loved by the Father that nothing will be withheld from you. He's teaching you discernment and perception. If it doesn't agree with what you hear in the silence, throw it out.

4. Record your dreams. The soul concerned with its own development not only learns from its dreams, but considers them essential to its own self-preservation, as I think I've said at least twice. It bears repeating.

5. Stand aside and see yourself go by. Recognize the universal law of cause and effect. Are you a walking, talking, human garbarge dump? Have your messiest thoughts taken on a life of their own? Is stuff coming out of your mouth that shames you? Do you see yourself doing unto

others before they do unto you? Congratulations! The turning and burning has begun. If you can see it, can perceive it in yourself, can recognize it for what it is, you now understand the universal law of like begets like, and you just graduated from being a victim to a survivor of your own past.

Now, maybe you're ready to become a *real* prophet.

18

Secrets of Spirit

In the same way an apple's seed is distinct from its peel, Spirit is distinct from soul.

The vastness of the idea of Spirit as the Life must be grasped before any comprehension of the interconnectedness to other souls, known as oneness, can be achieved.

Most basic is to first differentiate between *The* Spirit, the Holy Spirit or Holy Ghost, and spirits as entities or the spirit in which we do something.

In Chapter 6, "Secrets of the Soul's World," Spirit is described as the Creator's soul; the Father's soul; God's soul; the Universal soul; Life's soul; the soul of all Nature; Infinite Energy; the soul of the soul, yours and mine. In other words, you have a soul, I have a soul and the Creator

has a soul. Your soul has a soul; my soul has a soul, a tree
has a soul. The soul of your soul, the soul of my soul, the
soul of a tree, and the Creator's soul is the same soul. It is
the Spirit, who serves by giving life *nonselectively,* and is
feminine.

To clarify and amplify, this is the Spirit that moved in
Genesis 1:2. The Hebrew word is *rûwach*, which means
"wind breath, or a blast of breath, an exhalation." It is
associated with the ability to perceive oneself through the
senses, as a rational being, and "to make of quick understanding." Through *rûwach*, the mind knows itself to be.

By comparison, the definition of the *Holy Spirit* of the
New Testament comes from the Greek word *pneuma*, also
meaning "a current of air, breath, blast, or breeze," but is
associated with soul and Christ; "a spirit, by implication
vital principle, mental disposition, etc., or superhuman."
Pneuma comes from *pneumatikos*: "noncarnal, ethereal,
(divinely) supernatural, and regenerative." The Holy Spirit,
or Holy *pneuma*, is Christ's soul, and is masculine.

Also known as the Holy Ghost, the identical word,
pneuma, was translated into "ghost" instead of "spirit" in
some scriptures. Another name for the Holy Spirit, the
Comforter, (which is used only four times, all in Cayce's
favorite chapters, John 14, 15, and 16) comes from the
Greek word *parakletos*, meaning *intercessor* or *consoler.*
The Comforter is *the Spirit of Truth.*

Not true for the Hebrew *rûwach*, but included in the
definition for the Greek *pneuma*, are "demon" and
"demonic", implying that the potential for evil inherently
resides within the word "spirit." The inclusion of the word
"holy," which comes from the Greek *hagios* (and also
hagnos), which mean "sacred, blameless, consecrated, clean,
modest, perfect, chaste, clean, and pure," differentiates the
Holy Spirit, which is the soul of Christ, from a spirit of evil
intent. This, however, in no way implies that all spirit which
is not "holy" in the strictest sense is evil. *Rûwach* is the
breath of life itself. This indicates, rather, the degrees of the
implications behind the word "spirit." Thus the admoni-
tions of the Edgar Cayce readings (as well as the Bible, of

course) to "try the spirits." The destiny of the soul depends on knowing the difference.

Spirits may represent our own thoughts and ideas that masquerade as entities, but in some cases are actual entities. Often though, spirit reflects an attitude, such as the spirit in which we move about in the earth. To "live and move and have our being" in the mind of the Father, which is the Son, and the soul of the Son, which is the Holy Spirit, is the highest level of excellence attainable.

Cayce placed much emphasis on reading John 14-16, which explains, among other things, why Jesus had to leave before the Comforter, the Spirit of Truth, could come. The Spirit of Truth guides as we learn to discern, without judging, the spirits.

Discerning the Spirit

To discern someone's spirit means to perceive what's transpiring within. We do it every day in routine conversation with our associates. In each person standing before you the Spirit of God, which nonselectively animates all life in the Universe, is present. When Spirit leaves, life leaves. The soul of this person's soul is the same as your soul's soul. Therefore, judging another is like judging oneself, as all live because of Spirit. This is true even if the person standing before you is a mugger holding a knife. We are all interconnected through the soul-of-the-soul, even with the murderers on death row. We are interconnected to the vilest forms of human life of which we can conceive. We are also connected to one another's excellence in exactly the same way.

Therefore, what the Spirit of Truth shows us is a person's motivation. Learning to discern the motivating force behind words or actions is not the same as judging or condemning. It is more a matter of perceiving, and then understanding, their "spirit." It is a way of seeing our options concerning this person. Discernment carries over into our decisions and choices concerning organizations, groups, and ideas. Often though, understanding lags far behind perception. Though we may try to couple the faculty of reason with the intuitive faculty of discernment, reason may fail to "explain" the perception. This is when we say, "I don't know why, but I really do (or don't) feel comfortable with this person, organization, group, or idea."

It is equally important to discern the spirit in which we act. In the case of being faced by a mugger with a knife, the spirit in which we act may be in the spirit of the universal law of self-preservation. Under less extreme circumstances a more leisurely examination of our motivations concerning the various relationships which comprise society may prove revealing.

We only have to look around us to see what has been society's God. We only have to compare our society, which bows down to the god of technology, with, for instance, the Australian aborigines who, as a people, serve nature. But societal gods are insignificant when compared to each one's personal god or God.

It's almost impossible to live in this country without giving a passing nod to the Great Idol Commercialism, residing, we are told, on Madison Avenue in New York City. Its doctrine is simple: Buy or die a lonely death. Discerning the spirit behind the dogma is easy: manipulative greed. But the secret to who, what, and how Spirit moves lies less in the eyes that look outward on society and more in the eyes that look inward to the soul. Who but each one of us can discern whether we are in the world but not of the world? Only those special few we allow to look behind the mask.

But we know.

We know it if the spirit in which we act is giving back perfectly, deliciously indescribable, inexpressible moments of joy. The source of the joy reveals itself, forever bonding as precious memories that linger.

We also know if low spirits leave us empty, lonely, unfulfilled, and most of all *needy*.

Just as inner joy must be the hallmark of holiness, inner neediness must be the hallmark of unholiness. The hallmark of humanness must be that both can exist—not at the same time, but within the framework of the life being lived. This is why it's so important to discern the spirit in which we are moving ... and to let go of things and relationships that leave us needy. We must discern the motivation behind our actions and stop serving false gods.

The Spirit, the impelling influence of infinity, serves the Creator by animating all life throughout the universe. We become a servant to the Servant any time we act to further life. Our free will gives us the right to choose what form such actions shall take: anything done in the spirit of serving God through serving humanity, from sweeping streets to discovering the cure to cancer, and everything in between, can be considered creative service. It all depends on the spirit in which it is done. We serve the creation and the Creator—and ourselves—when we serve one another.

Spirit Contrasted with Soul

There is a vast difference between spirit and soul.

Unlike Spirit, the soul does develop. In much the same way the human mind develops as it opens itself to knowledge, the soul develops as it opens itself to the unseen. The Spirit has no need to develop. It is the same yesterday, today, and tomorrow.

The Spirit cannot die or be separated from the Maker. The soul can. Soul, like the apple's peel, will wither and disappear if Spirit leaves it. The soul gives life to the flesh and blood body, but Spirit gives life to the soul.

Spirit, the soul of Life, is nonselective. Spirit animates all life—that perceived as good, as well as that perceived as evil.

Soul, however, is selective. Soul can and must choose— through its free-will mind—how it will end up. The soul's experience "must be finished before the entity may either be blotted out or come into full brotherhood. . . .'' The soul can will its own banishment, said Cayce.

Spirit is like electricity, music and mathematics in that it simply exists in the universe. The soul lives through the power of Spirit, but is "transformed" through mind. The ideal is the transformer/conductor of Spirit. It could be said, then, that Spirit becomes Holy Spirit when it is transformed through Christ mind.

Just as lights shine on earth because the proper electrical connection has been made, so shines the soul in the universe, when the Ideal is being lived.

Appendix

Research for this book has convinced me that we who live in Spiritville, Planet Earth—all citizens of the same realm—can barely communicate with one another because we don't speak the same language. We may be saying the same thing, yet be tripping over semantics.

How can we know whether we agree when we can't get past the language barrier? How can we help one another if we don't understand each other?

For a writer, the problem of painting a picture of the secrets of the universe using mere words is like an artist trying to capture the aurora borealis using mere paint. The Edgar Cayce readings are like a series of stop-motion photographs of the northern lights, each one significant to the picture, but not the whole picture. Only through patient,

deliberate analysis does one become aware of and comfortable with the undulations, and the shifts and blendings of
shapes and colors. Comfortable in the sense of not fearing
the motion, as some Eskimos do, but rather, comfortable with
the awe-inspiring fascination that occurs with the phenomenon. But just as scientists have found that the secrets to
the electrical patterns of earth lie within the activity of the
aurora, researchers who not only study but test the concepts
have discovered that the secrets to the spiritual universe lie
within the Edgar Cayce readings.

As a student, these secrets, I discovered, reside within
four overlapping areas: heredity, environment, mind, and
spirit.[1] Individually, we are the sum total of these four
influences on three levels: physical, mental, and spiritual.

Grouped here for reference are the briefest definitions for
the twelve elements that comprise life, plus various Trinities
mentioned in the readings.

In the footnotes, the reference to the Book number
indicates in which of the twenty-two currently available
Library Series books the reading is found. Some readings
are included in more than one book because of their multi-
ple categorical interest.

Reading numbers and notes are included in the footnotes
for the benefit of the serious student.

Terms

Heredity

1. PHYSICAL LEVEL OF HEREDITY: Lineage/genetics.
2. MENTAL LEVEL OF HEREDITY: Total of what mind
has built since the beginning.
3. SPIRITUAL LEVEL OF HEREDITY: Total of what soul
has done with what mind has built.
   Trinity
   FATHER, The Maker.
   SON, The mind of Father.
   HOLY GHOST, The soul of Son.[2]

[1](See 281-24, Book 17, p. 278.)
[2](See 1742-4, A-1, Book 16, p. 373).

Environment

4. PHYSICAL LEVEL OF ENVIRONMENT: Materiality.
5. MENTAL LEVEL OF ENVIRONMENT: What mind perceives.
6. SPIRITUAL LEVEL OF ENVIRONMENT: What soul experiences.[3]

Trinity
BODY: The physical body.
MIND: The mind of body.
SOUL: The soul of body.

Mind

7. PHYSICAL LEVEL OF MIND: Consciousness while awake.
8. MENTAL LEVEL OF MIND: Subconscious collection of self-knowledge.
9. SPIRITUAL LEVEL OF MIND: Superconscious collection of all knowledge.[4]

Trinity
LIFE: That which the Maker made.
CHRIST: The mind of the Maker.
SPIRIT: The soul of the Maker.

Spirit

10. PHYSICAL LEVEL OF SPIRIT: The body of soul.
11. MENTAL LEVEL OF SPIRIT: The mind of soul.
12. SPIRITUAL LEVEL OF SPIRIT: The soul of soul.

Trinity
GOD: That which the Maker made Himself.
JESUS: The mind of GOD.
MARY: The soul of GOD.

The research revealed a more complex view of life than the one commonly represented by pyramidal modeling.

[3](See 826-11, Book 20, p. 114. This reading is important in many ways.)

[4]See 900-21, A-1&2, Book 20, p. 11. Shows three levels of mind *in man*, plus one outside of man. See also 3744-1, Book 20, p. 11 for two mind forces; also, comment on animals having soul and spirit, but not subconscious mind. Reading 5749-3, A-5, speaks of an *outer* consciousness.)

The spiritual universe of humankind is ordinarily thought of as being comprised of one "trinity" known as Physical, Mental, and Spiritual, which is sitting on a four-square base of Heredity, Environment, Mind, and Spirit. This concept can be modeled pyramidally, but is actually a limited representation of human life.

The following models borrow the popular abbreviation *PMS* to represent Physical, Mental and Spiritual.

THE PYRAMIDAL MODEL OF HUMANKIND VIEWED FROM ABOVE

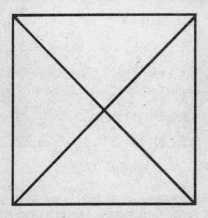

The following model represents human life on earth more accurately. It is composed of three squares, one each for the Physical, Mental, and Spiritual levels. An additional abbreviation, HEMS, is employed to represent Heredity, Environment, Mind, and Spirit.

The three squares are superimposed onto one another, forming a twelve-pointed star. As with any model which attempts to separate the influences that comprise consciousness, this one limits the concept, and fails to demonstrate the complexity of the soul evolving and Spirit involving.

We have used three shadings to clarify which square represents which level. No particular significance is implied by the strength of the shadings.

THE TWELVE-POINTED STAR MODEL

An attempt to demonstrate motion would likely confuse the picture rather than clarify. However, the student may bring his or her own comprehension of motion by imagining the star separating into a sort of spiraling staircase: the soul spiraling or stair-stepping heavenward and Spirit spiraling or stair-stepping earthward simultaneously.

In the previous model the four corners of the three squares represent Heredity, Environment, Mind, and Spirit on three levels: Physical, Mental, and Spiritual.

However, the following model eliminates HEMS, only for the sake of clarity. But before leaving the acronym, it is worth noting that ''hems'' are *borders*. We often feel ''hemmed in'' by our borders of heredity and environment and perhaps mind and spirit also. We seek to expand our borders, to transcend the limits of human existence, to move beyond self into that which we perceive to be limitless. In other words, we seek the way home. But Cayce said our limitations are self-created by what has been our ideal. Often we feel lost. We wander aimlessly, not knowing if the way home is inward or outward. The Edgar Cayce readings indicate it is both: inward to the Christ and outward to our fellow humans. And both directions involve and employ the senses to light the path.

When each of the three squares are halved to become six triangles, the triangles represent humanity's five senses plus the sixth sense, which is seen in Chapter 6, "Secrets of the Soul's World," to be more than merely intuitive. The PMS levels are retained.

THE SENSES[5]

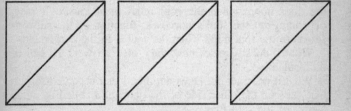

Body, Mind, Soul, and Spirit[6]— Traits of Each

The sections of a grapefruit are part of the whole fruit, but separating the sections makes it easier to eat. Likewise,

[5](Cayce may have been referring to the senses when he spoke of the "sextette." See 5747-2, A-3, Book 12, p. 227.)

[6](See 3357-2, Book 20, near the bottom of p. 13.)

bite-size chunks of information are easier to digest, though they belong to the whole. Therefore, because confusion among the various aspects of body, mind, soul, and spirit hinders some of us, the following may be helpful.

As Cayce told one woman, even though we know ourselves to be body, mind, and soul, we need to be on "speaking terms even with that which is a universal consciousness."[7] No attempt has been made to incorporate other names and definitions from sources other than the Edgar Cayce readings, except for Carl Jung's references to the collective."

Spiritual Level of Mind

Other Names: Superconscious; The Mind of God; The Mind of the Father; Universal Mind; Christ Mind; The Divide; The Lamb; The Shepherd; The Door; The Way; The I Am; Our Mind, the Son;[8] The Collective Unconscious.[9]

What it is: Created and creative; the first creation; the collection of all knowledge since the beginning; the barrier the soul's mind must cross to reach oneness; also known as the door upon which the soul mind must knock; it may, depending on the soul's purposes, function as the subconscious to the soul mind when the soul is in the borderlands.

What it does: Creates new stars, etc.; answers the call of the soul mind.

What it does not do: Does not die; does not force itself on us; waits on the other side of the door until called by some aspect of the soul mind.

[7](See 954-5, Book 16, p. 92.)

[8](See 1567-2, Book 1, p. 63.)

[9](See 262-80, Book 20, p. 14, for a reference to "group mind" of the plant, mineral, and animal kingdoms. Group soul or consciousness is also mentioned. See also 4083-1, Book 20, p. 4. See also *Meditation and the Mind of Man*, p. 72, for the chart showing the "collective unconscious.")

Mental Level of Spirit[10]

Other Names: Soul mind; Body-mind of the soul.[11]

What it is: Memory;[12] the free-will mind of each individual soul, awakened to oneness by the creative conscience,[13] which chooses whether to be guided by, in order to join and become one with, the Spiritual Spirit; where the Christ pattern is imprinted.

What it does: Dreams; elects whether to be developed and by whom or what; is selective; may, depending on the soul's purposes, become the consciousness in the borderland; can act for and choose between both good and evil; can move toward or away from its Creator; can opt for life or death; can both sleep and die, be banished, banish itself, or be blotted out.[14]

*Note: This is where "oneness" can happen. The Soul Mind elects to surrender itself to the soul's soul, which is the same as God's soul. See below.

What it does not do: Maintain its individuality eternally unless it chooses.

Spiritual Level of Spirit

Other Names: Universal Soul; Soul-of-the-Soul; Oversoul;[15] God's Soul; Life's Soul; Infinite Energy; The Spirit; The Servant; The Collective Soul; the First Cause.

What it is: Your soul's soul, my soul's soul, God's soul.[16] It is the same soul. That which develops soul's mind.

What it does: Impels infinity; activates and animates all Mind's creations and life nonselectively; develops the Soul Mind when asked; helps the soul mind to cross the divide known as the Superconscious.

[10](Sin happened in spirit first. See 1602-3, Book 20, p. 8. Also "attributes of mind are a portion of the soul." See 240-2, Book 16, p. 447.)

[11](See 275-36, Book 20, p. 212.)

[12](Memory is the mind of the soul. See 137-25, Book 20, pp. 93-94.)

[13](See 696-3, Book 20, p. 94 and 254-54, A-5, Book 20, p. 93.)

[14](See 4083-1, 3003-1, 900-20, 3744-2, A-22, 826-8.)

[15](The soul comes from a soul. See 815-7, Book 17, p. 448.)

[16](See 900-89, A-12 & 13, Book 16, p. 407.)

What it does not do: Does not develop (no need to); does not sleep or die, but may eventually withdraw from a soul who wishes it so.

Physical Level of Spirit[17]

Other Names: Soul-Body; Body-Soul; Individuality (actually refers to entire soul); Spiritual Body; Body-Spiritual; Other Self; Dream Self; Real Self; Astral Body; Cosmic Body; Cosmic Consciousness; Etheric Body; Body of the Thought Forms.[18]

What it is: The eternal, invisible something; associated with the real desire, imagination, habits; can share some of the same attributes as the subconscious; the vessel of the soul's mind and the soul's soul; that which expresses the soul mind.[19]

What it does: Houses the individual soul mind; becomes visible in lucid moments of awareness of its relationship to the mental and physical body; concerns itself with the ideal; gives the Spiritual Spirit a form in which to work; acts as a receptor for the Infinite Energy; activates the flesh and blood body through the endocrine system; experiences sleep, separation, and banishment, or eternal life.

What it does not do: Maintain its individuality eternally unless the Soul Mind chooses.[20]

Physical Level of Mind

Other names: Consciousness; Physical Conscious.[21]

What it is: Physical awareness.

What it does: Receives input from the six senses; interacts

---

[17](That built by thought and deed—active particles, atoms—makes up the soul body. See 5756-4, Book 16, p. 50. See also 1632-2, Book 20, p. 209, last graf.)

[18](See 275-36, Book 20, p. 212 and 696-3, Book 20, p. 94.)

[19](Soul body becomes what the mind thinks upon. That is destiny. See 262-78, Book 20, p. 25, and 900-147, Book 20, p. 38, A-12.)

[20](Soul body may or may not be controlled by the good or *bad* influences of spirit. See 2067-1, Book 16, p. 51-52.)

[21](See 5752-3.)

with the subconscious; also receives input from the soul's mind and the soul's soul:

Input...Input

Six Senses --------›Physical Mind‹--------Soul's Soul

-------------------------------- + --------------------------------

The point where the two meet is transformation.

Note that input from the soul's mind does not effect transformation as the soul's mind can refuse to surrender to the soul's soul. Oneness originates at the level of the soul's soul, which is one soul. The sixth sense is more accurately associated with the soul's mind.

What it does: both sleeps (is laid aside during sleep) and dies.

What it does not do: Live eternally.

Mental Level of Mind

Other Names: Subconscious, Unconscious; Underconscious; Unconscious Conscious.[22]

What it is: The storehouse of every act, thought, or deed, all patterned responses of the past, such as addictions and habits,[23] of all memory, both relevant and irrelevant; where ego-self lives.

What it does: Interacts with physical and soul minds; may interact with dreams;[24] reacts according to past pattern; tries to maintain its authority; where the battle between spirit and flesh is fought; may, depending on the soul's purposes, become the soul's consciousness in the borderlands; can learn new responses.

[22](See Book 20, 3744-1, p. 11; 5752-3, p. 41, which very clearly speaks of three levels of consciousness within the individual, plus the Creative Forces, as well as the "degrading" forces.)

[23](See 900-20, Book 17, p. 176 and 900-21, A-2, Book 20, p. 12: The subconscious has the storing of knowledge.)

[24](See 136-54, Book 20, p. 234: To the subconscious there is no past or future, all present.)

What it does not do: Surrender without a fight.

Physical Level of Body

Other Names: Vessel; The Temple; Body-Physical; Material Body.

What it is: Miniature Universe of cells, each of which is a miniature universe; a corpuscle in the body of God.

What it does: Houses the mental and soul bodies; responds to adherence to or breaking of universal laws governing nature; associated with human desires and appetites; becomes that which is assimilated from the material; exists in time and space while Spirit gives life to cells; both sleeps and dies.

What it does not do: Live eternally.

Mental Level of Body[25]

Other Names: Body-Mental; Mind-Body; Body-Mind.

What it is: That directing influence of the physical, mental, and spiritual functions, emotions and manifestations; becomes that which is assimilated from both the physical mind and soul mind;[26] associated with the senses and with desire.[27]

What it does: Determines conduct and actions concerning self, others, things, conditions, and circumstances; builds both physically and spiritually, but must manifest materially.

What it does not do: Live eternally unless soul mind chooses.[28]

Universal Level of Body

Other Names: The Universe; Universal Vessel.

What it is: The outer limits of creation.

What it does: Houses all creation.

---

[25](See 1631-1, Book 20, p. 209 and 531-4, Book 20, p. 24.)
[26](See 2475-1, Book 20, p. 211.)
[27](See 276-7, Book 20, p. 206.)
[28](See 5118-1, Book 20, bottom of p. 16, mind's limitations.)

What it does not do: Emcompass or contain the entire Mind or Spirit of the Creator.

To Summarize

There are *four* levels of "body." The three of them associated with humankind live within the universal body of God.[29]

1. Universal Body.
2. Individual Physical Body.
3. Individual Mental Body.
4. Individual Soul Body.

There are *four* levels of "mind," three of them individual, one universal.[30]

1. Universal Mind
2. Individual Physical Mind.
3. Individual Mental Mind.
4. Individual Soul Mind.

There are *two* parts to the individual soul.[31]

1. Soul Body.
2. Soul Mind.

The third part of the individual soul is the *one* Spirit.[32]
There is *one* "Spirit."

1. Universal or Spiritual Spirit.

All other "spirit" labels merely attempt to describe the invisible nature of the spiritual element.

There is *one* God.

1. God the Father, or Creator.

Again, we have twelve knowable elements of human life. These twelve, plus the twelve composed of the Physical, Mental, and Spiritual elements of Heredity, Environment, Spirit, and Mind, total twenty-four which corresponds to the "four and twenty elders" seated around the place where we

---

[29](See 267-2, A-7, Book 20, p. 206 and 1632-1, Book 20, p. 209.)

[30](See 5752-3, Book 20, p. 41, where it speaks of how man's finite mind became separated. See also 900-21, A-2, Book 20, p. 12.)

[31](The soul has a body, mind, and soul. See 4083-1, A-9, Book 20, p. 7. See also 2246-1, Book 16, p. 305, where it says the soul is the image of the Maker, not the body.)

[32](See 900-89, A-12 & 13, Book 16, p. 407.)

meet with the Father, the "throne" of Revelation 4:4. And the secrets of numbers begin to unfold.

But that will have to be another book.

"For knowledge alone makes one mad..."
—311-7[33]

Definitions of Universal Laws

Law of Attraction: We draw, by some mysterious force, people, places, things, circumstances, and situations that appeal either in a negative or positive way to the emotions or senses. In physics, the law of attraction is the electric or magnetic force that acts between oppositely charged bodies, tending to draw them together. In spiritual development, we may keep attracting the same conditions again and again until we have neutralized the magnetic field by finally learning the lesson the condition would teach us.

Law of Like Begets Like: We "father" that which is like us. We procreate, generate, and cause all the good that is happening to us—as well as that perceived as "bad."

Law of Cause and Effect: For every action there is a direct reaction. There is a relationship between actions or events in that one or more are always the result of the other or others. Also known as "as ye sow so shall ye reap"; the law of karma; the law of reciprocity; the law of the tenfold return; law of abundance; law of stewardship; law of recompense.[34]

Law of Self-Preservation: The preservation of oneself from harm or destruction.

Law of Grace and Mercy: Grace is immunity and unmerited favor. Mercy is a reprieve from a fate of considerable severity without further implication. The law of grace and mercy, then, is *another chance.* Expressed best in the golden rule: Do unto others as you would have them do unto you.

[33](Book 17, p. 499.)
[34](Law of recompense, Book 16, p. 110, 5332-1.)

Law of Expectancy: Some degree of what we look forward to or regard as likely to happen, anticipate the occurrence or the coming of, eventually happens.

Law of Consistency: Behavior agreed upon and deemed necessary by at least two of the three levels of self, and if acted out regularly, produces a feeling of well-being and peace.

Law of One: There is one God, and we the created are one people who live through the one spirit, the soul of God.

Law of Truth: The truth shall make you free.

Law of Love: Giving with gratitude.

And finally...

...reading the Edgar Cayce readings verbatim is like crossing the mountains in a covered wagon. You know there's gold in them there hills, but Lord, are you going to live long enough to find it?

The peaks and valleys jostle your insides and jiggle your brain. A magic carpet would be nice, to just more or less float over the scene, observing what we will. But real treasure is always hidden. We have to dig for it. It's like we're in a big game of hide-and-seek with God. Only it isn't a game. This life isn't a rehearsal for the next one. This one counts.

Some of the information contained in this book suggests we're coming to the end of this trail, that the jig is about to be up. This book has been written as an inner map, a guide to the secret treasure within you. It is only hoped that it has not left your personal life untouched.

As a mapmaker I have trudged some of the terrain of the Cayce readings. But there is far too much for one miner to haul out alone. I have traced the terrain onto these pages as best I can, knowing that when you journey there yourself, you will discover beauties I have missed. I have taken away only that which I could carry, that which my eyes could see and my arms could hold. I bring it to you and place it before you as a gift. Take what you will, use what you need, give it away, and it will come back to you multiplied.

Just as no mapmaker can present the whole picture, no

markings on a page can show you the beauty of the mountains until you go there yourself. You have to involve all of your senses—smell them, taste them, touch them, hear them speak to you in their own voice. But I entreat you to go and see what I've seen, feel what I've felt, be where I've been. The view is glorious, and the trip is one-way.

The paraphrasing of the readings is meant to smooth out some of the pebbles along the trail. I can only hope I have not mistaken a golden nugget for a pebble and omitted it inadvertently in the narrative. If I have, the old-timers will catch me at it and forgive me; the newcomers will understand that trying to write it is as hard as trying to live it. For this journey can only be lived one day at a time—occasionally, one hour or moment at a time. The wheels fall off the wagon; savages attack; fallen timber blocks our path. But we get there. Sometimes beaten. Sometimes bloody for the effort. Often too tired to appreciate how far we've come. But we get there, often leaning on the arm of someone we've helped, and He is there to say, "Well done."

What else is there?

THE A.R.E. TODAY

The Association for Research and Enlightenment, Inc., is a non-profit, open membership organization committed to spiritual growth, holistic healing, psychical research and its spiritual dimensions; and more specifically, to making practical use of the psychic readings of the late Edgar Cayce. Through nationwide programs, publications and study groups, A.R.E. offers all those interested practical information and approaches for individual study and application to better understand and relate to themselves, to other people and to the universe. A.R.E. membership and outreach is concentrated in the United States with growing involvement throughout the world.

The headquarters at Virginia Beach, Virginia, includes a library/conference center, administrative offices and publishing facilities, and are served by a beachfront motel. The library is one of the largest metaphysical, parapsychological libraries in the country. A.R.E. operates a bookstore, which also offers mail-order service and carries approximately 1,000 titles on nearly every subject related to spiritual growth, world religions, parapsychology and transpersonal psychology. A.R.E. serves its members through nationwide lecture programs, publications, a Braille library, a camp and an extensive Study Group Program.

The A.R.E. facilities, located at 67th Street and Atlantic Avenue, are open year-round. Visitors are always welcome and may write A.R.E., P.O. Box 595, Virginia Beach, VA 23451, for more information about the Association.